THE
WATER BEETLE

BY NANCY MITFORD

Illustrated by

OSBERT LANCASTER

New York   1986   *Atheneum*

TO
VIOLET HAMMERSLEY

Library of Congress Cataloging-in-Publication Data
Mitford, Nancy, 1904-1973.
The water beetle.
I. Title.
PR6025.I88W3   1986   824'.914   85-28710
ISBN 0-689-70703-7

Manufactured by Fairfield Graphics
Fairfield, Pennsylvania
First Atheneum Paperback Edition

THE WATER BEETLE

BOOKS BY NANCY MITFORD

The water beetle here shall teach
A lesson far beyond your reach.
She aggravates the human race
By gliding on the water's face
Assigning each to each its place.
But if she ever stopped to think
Of how she did it, she would sink.

> *Moral*
> Don't ask questions.

—After HILAIRE BELLOC
(The Moral Alphabet)

ACKNOWLEDGEMENTS

'Portrait of a French Country House', 'Blor', 'Wicked Thoughts in Greece' and 'In Defence of Louis XV' originally appeared in the *Sunday Times*, and 'Reading for Pleasure', which was originally entitled 'A Taste of Honey', is reprinted by permission of *The Times*.

'The Great Little Duke' first appeared in the *New Statesman*, 'The Tourist' was first printed in *Encounter*, and 'Augustus Hare, 1834–1903' was originally published in *Horizon*.

'Chic' is reprinted by permission of the *Atlantic Monthly*, and 'Some Rooms for Improvement' appeared in America in *Horizon*.

CONTENTS

Part One
ENGLISH

Part Two
FOREIGN

Part One

ENGLISH

Blor

UNLIKE my sister Diana, who declares (and she is rather a truthful person) that she remembers having a bottle, I can remember almost nothing about my early childhood. It is shrouded in a thick mist which seldom lifts except on the occasion of some public event. For instance, I see our dining-room at 1 Graham Street (now Graham Terrace), the house where I was born; my father and mother, at breakfast, are reading newspapers with black edges to them and they are both crying. The tears startle me—so does the news; the King is dead. The King was Edward VII. Now, the funny thing about this mental tableau is that, whereas in fact my parents were beautiful and young at the time, aged 30 and 31, they appear in it as two old people, contemporaries of the King whom they mourn. The room, the wallpaper (white with a green wreath round the cornice), the street outside and the black-edged *Times* are a real image; the two living creatures are seen subjectively and I very much doubt if those tears really flowed at all. So much for my memory.

Soon after this we moved to Victoria Road. Another tableau: walking towards the Park I am saying to Blor, who is pushing one or two of my sisters in a pram: 'How big is the *Titanic*?' 'As big as from here to Kensy High Street.' To this day I see the *Titanic* as Victoria Road, houses, trees and all, steaming through the icebergs. Its sinking

3

gave me ideas, of a rather dreadful kind, I am sorry to say. My father and mother used to go every other year to Canada in order to prospect for gold. Poor but optimistic, they were quite sure that sooner or later their ship would come home. But I became very hopeful that on one of these journeys their ship would go down; then, no doubt, like Katy in *What Katy Did*, I would gather up the reins of the household in small but capable hands and boss 'the others'. (It never occurred to me that, in fact, some uncle or aunt would no doubt take us over and boss us all). I remember scanning Blor's *Daily News* for an account of the shipwreck: 'Mr and Mrs Mitford are among the regretted victims.' I knew this delightful day dream would never come true; no doubt if it had I would have been as sad as one can be at seven years old, because in fact I loved my parents, while later in life all my faults and disabilities would have been put down to this early tragedy.

By far the most vivid of my fitful recollections is the outbreak of war in 1914. When it appeared to be imminent Blor told me to pray for peace. But I thought, if we had war, England might be invaded; then, like Robin Hood, one would take to the greenwood tree and somehow or another manage to kill a German. It was more than I could do to pray for peace. I prayed, as hard as I could, for war. I knew quite well how wicked this was; when my favourite uncle was killed I had terrible feelings of guilt.

My prayer having been granted as prayers so often are, I was soon sitting like a *tricoteuse*, on the balcony of Grandfather Redesdale's house in Kensy High Street, crocheting an endless purple scarf while the troops marched by on their way to France. (There was no khaki wool to be had so early in the war—you took what you could get.) I

and the others, Pam, Tom and Diana, Blor and Ada, the
nursery maid, were staying with my grandfather because my
mother was, as usual, increasing the number of the others,
an occupation which I thought extremely unnecessary. On
8th August a girl was born; she was christened Unity, after
an actress my mother admired called Unity Moore, and
Valkyrie after the war maidens. This was Grandfather
Redesdale's idea; he said these maidens were not German
but Scandinavian. He was a great friend of Wagner's and
must have known. Then we all went back to Victoria Road.
The war turned out to be less exciting than I had hoped,
though we did see the Zeppelin come down in flames at
Potters Bar. I fell in love with Captain Platt in my father's
regiment, an important General of the next war, and
crocheted end ess pairs of khaki mittens for him—I am not
sure that they were inflicted on him. In any case, all this
crocheting was the nearest I ever got to killing an enemy, a
fact which I am still regretting.

I don't remember much more of my early childhood;
what I am now going to recount mostly comes from family
hearsay. Our first Nanny was Lily Kersey; 'Ninny Kudgey',
daughter of the captain of Grandfather Bowles's yacht.
My mother adored the sea, which she saw in terms of
Tissot rather than Conrad; she christened me Nancy in the
hopes that a sailor's wife a sailor's star I'd be; she gave me
in charge of Ninny so that a love of ocean waves should
be implanted in my young psychology. It all turned out
rather differently, however. Ninny was quite untrained
and knew nothing about babies; she laid the foundations of
the low stamina which has always been such a handicap to
me in life. I think she was also partly responsible for my
great nastiness to the others. My next sister Pam was born

three days before my third birthday; Ninny Kudgey instantly transferred her affections. My mother used to hear me saying, 'Oh Ninny how I wish you could still love me!' In the end, she says, I became too sad and Ninny was sent away. But she was succeeded by the Unkind Nanny. The Unkind Nanny is a legendary figure in the family. Had we been slightly older she might well have found herself the biter bit, but it must be borne in mind that at this time I was between three and six and the others between nothing and three. I am not quite sure what form the unkindness took. I, of course, cannot remember; the others were really too little (Diana, the great rememberer, was only four months old when she left) and my mother seems to have a certain feeling of guilt which prevents her from discussing the subject. Did the Nanny beat us or starve us or merely refuse to laugh at our jokes? I shall never know. Another thing, like the False Dimitris there may have been more than one Unkind Nanny, though this is not certain. In short, the three years after the departure of Ninny Kudgey were a kind of Mitford dark ages, full of mystery, wickedness and horror. No reliable records exist of this period and we turn our minds from it with relief. During it, Tom was born and then Diana.

My mother has always lived in a dream world of her own and no doubt was even dreamier during her many pregnancies. Later in life she has taken to reading, preferring, like Mr Raymond Mortimer, books about Victorian clergymen to any others, so that my biographies are not much good to her. But when she was young she never opened a book and it is difficult to imagine what her tastes and occupations may have been. My father and she disliked society, or thought they did—there again, later on they rather took to

it—and literally never went out. She had no cooking or
housework to do. In those days you might be considered
very poor by comparison with other people of the same sort
and yet have five servants in a tiny house. How different are
the lives of such young couples now! Last time I was in
London I met a friend pushing her granddaughter round
Eaton Square in a pram. We chatted for a while; the wind
was bitter; I said: 'Why don't we go and put our toes in the
nursery fender and let Nanny give us some tea?' 'There is
no nursery, there is no fender, there is no Nanny.' We took
the baby home and handed it over to an Italian girl who was
ironing in the drawing-room; no fire; indeed no fireplace.
It had been turned into a cupboard for hunting-boots.

So what did my mother do all day? She says now, when
cross-examined, that she lived for us. Perhaps she did, but
nobody could say that she lived with us. It was not the cus-
tom then. I think that nothing in my life has changed more
than the relationship between mothers and young children. In those days a distance was always kept. Even so she
was perhaps abnormally detached. On one occasion Unity
rushed into the drawing-room, where she was at her
writing-table, saying: 'Muv, Muv, Decca is standing on the
roof—she says she's going to commit suicide!' 'Oh, poor
duck,' said my mother, 'I hope she won't do anything so
terrible' and went on writing.

We were looked after by a nurse and nursery maid; we
'came down' to see our parents finishing their breakfast and
again, dressed up in party clothes, after tea. Occasionally, of
course, there were treats; we went to Gorringes or the Zoo,
or an aunt or uncle took us to a pantomime, after which, all
having fallen desperately in love with some character on the
stage, we would be insupportable for weeks. But we spent

7

the major part of our lives in the nursery. My mother says she has forgotten how she found out about the Unkind Nanny's (or Nannies') unkindness. Little children, of course, never tell tales about those in authority. Perhaps the neighbours sent for the police, but I don't think so. Even I would have noticed the irruption of a bobby in the nursery, I suppose. The house was minute; probably my parents, having heard unmistakable sounds of torture going on upstairs for a few months, decided that the time had come for another change. I do vaguely remember the sacking of the Nanny. My mother retired to bed, as she often did when things became dramatic, leaving my father to perform the execution. There was a confrontation in the nursery as of two mastodons; oddly enough, throughout the terrifying battle which ensued, I felt entirely on the side of the Nanny.

It took my mother some time to find a successor. She had no wish to fall upon another False Dimitri; she longed to finish bringing up her children with no more changes. She interviewed about a dozen nurses, including one with the almost irresistible name of Lily Duck. When she saw Blor, who was 39, she thought her too old and frail to look after a large and growing family. Blor herself wondered whether she could manage to push a pram, with two children and a sort of *strapontin* for a third, all the way from Graham Street to the Park. However, when she saw the baby, Diana, all these doubts vanished. 'I can see her face now,' says my mother, 'as she said, "Oh! what a lovely baby!"' So she moved into our family and never moved out again. Of course, I can remember nothing of all this; it happened just before my sixth birthday. I was reading *Ivanhoe*, so Blor has often told me, and my furious little round face was concealed behind the book as she took off hat and cape for the first

'I was reading *Ivanhoe*. . . .'

time, in our nursery. I remember every word of *Ivanhoe*, which I have never read since, but have no recollection of the advent of Blor. No doubt it seemed at once as though she had been with us for ever.

Her name was Laura Dicks and she came from Egham. Charming to look at, she had a kind, white face, with curly reddish-brown hair. Out of doors she wore a bonnet, of shiny black straw trimmed with a velvet bow and strings. The French painter Helleu used to say he could live in London if only because of the bonnets of the Nannies in the Park. When Blor changed her flat bow for a velvet ruche, Diana, who was about two, says she noticed it and cried. Mr Dicks, the father of Blor, looked like God the Father with a long white beard; he was a smith—he made wrought-iron gates and grew black pansies. Her many brothers and sisters looked like her. They were all clever and had successful careers. The family was advanced in its views, liberal and non-conformist, very different from the one in which she was to spend the rest of her life. My parents were ultraconservative and Church of England, with the emphasis on England. They went to church regularly, in order to support the State; I doubt if either of them ever had a conventionally religious thought. Indeed, my mother used to say: But what happens when people pray? How can they think of enough things to ask for? Somebody once told her about the resurrection of the body and she became quite hysterical at the idea; in spite of the fact that she proclaimed her belief in it, out loud, every Sunday, she had not considered its strange implications. Blor stuck to her guns and never changed her way of thinking. She was very religious and I believed she suffered from not being able to go to her own church during the months, sometimes years, on end that we lived in the country. She attended the village church and she asked Mr Ward, our vicar, if she could take Communion there, but he was obliged to say no. When the Liberal Party declined, Blor took to voting Labour, to the horror of my sisters. 'How did you vote, Blor?'

'Well, darling, to vote for the Liberal candidate would only put in the Conservative, you know.'

'Blor! Never tell me you voted for the Socialists?'

'Yes, darling, that's just what I did.'

'Oh! You are naughty! What will the Führer say?'

Even I, who voted Labour myself, felt rather shocked. Such frivolities seemed unsuitable for Blor.

However, she is one of the few people with whom none of us ever had a political quarrel—or indeed a quarrel of any sort. The strong passions that raged in our house were kept on the other side of the nursery door; even my father, armed with hunting crop or croquet mallet, in pursuit of a screaming but delighted quarry, would go so far and no further. Somehow the egg-shell skull of the current baby was protected from its rampaging relations by Blor's personality. She had a wonderful capacity for taking things as they came and a very English talent for compromise. In two respects she was unlike the usual Nanny. We were never irritated by tales of paragons she had been with before us; and she always got on quite well with our governesses, upholding their authority as she did that of our parents. When we grew up she never interfered in our lives. If she disapproved of something one said or did, she would shrug her shoulders and make a little sound between a sniff and clearing her throat. She hardly ever spoke out—perhaps never—and on the whole our vagaries were accepted with no more stringent comment than 'Hm'—

sniff—'very *silly*, darling.' A strong Puritan streak made her despise pleasure. Her father disapproved of the theatre and she had never seen the inside of one until I badgered and wheedled my mother to let me go to the Opera. I was fifteen and under the influence of Tolstoy's novels at the time. The word Opera to me signified the World in all its wickedness and glamour; nothing to do with the performance, of course—I was after the House, with its boxes, its foyer and its coulisses, gallant men in opera hats and lovely women in opera cloaks, gazing at each other through opera glasses. Blor and I went off together to a matinée of *Faust*, at Oxford. I need say no more.

When we left the schoolroom and began to live for pleasure its occupational complaints got no sympathy from Blor. One tottered, lean and pale, into the nursery, having danced until dawn: 'Oh, Blor I'm so tired!' The reply was: 'I don't pity you!' My first ball dress was viewed without enthusiasm. 'You'll be cold.' On Diana's wedding day, when she was trying to arrange her veil to its best effect, Blor remarked: 'Don't worry, darling—nobody's going to look at *you*.'

She once said to Unity: 'I do wish you wouldn't keep going to Germany, darling.'

'Why, Blor?'

Sniff. 'All those men!'

What could be more descriptive of Hitler's Germany?

When Diana's boys began using four-letter words Blor said: 'I'm afraid nobody will like them when they are grown up if that's how they talk!'

My mother, whose views on health were rudimentary, who had never heard of hygiene and did not really believe in illness, had one medical superstition which nothing could shake. Pig, she thought, was unclean and, like the Jews and the Arabs, we were strictly forbidden to eat it. The perfect health of Arabs is a very current English belief. How many times have I been told not to expose myself to the sun because they wear blankets in heat-waves! (Most of those I see are noticeable for their poor physique, but let that pass.) Of course, we don't go so far as to copy their ablutions; true cleanliness is considered rather immoral by my compatriots, who lie for hours in hot baths, but are maddened at the sight of a bidet.

The ruling that deprived us children of pig also forbade horse and oysters; that was not a real hardship, because no other member of the family ate horse, and oysters are seldom seen in the Cotswolds. But pig! Whiffs of fried bacon from my father's breakfast and the sight of him tucking into sausage rolls or sausage mash, cold gammon and cranberry sauce, pork chops with apple sauce, pigs' thinkers and trotters and Bath chaps were daily tortures; the occasional sucking-pig which crackled into the dining-room hardly bears contemplating, even now. Our craving for the stuff amounted to an obsession. Others have told how my young sisters were to be seen concealing sausages up their knickers and running off to eat them in some secluded spot; the first letter my brother Tom wrote from his private school simply stated 'We have sossages every day.' Blor must have thought this 'no pig' rule eccentric, if not rather mad; she never commented on it and always upheld it, except on one occasion. She and convalescent Debo were sent to a seaside hotel for a breezy fortnight. Ordering luncheon on the first day Debo said to the waiter, in what she thought was a grown-up voice: 'I'll have a very little bit of ham.' Then she looked at Blor to see what the reaction would be. Blor gave her disapproving sniff, but she only said: 'Well, it must be a very, very little bit of ham.'

My parents, as is only human, had favourites among their daughters. Tom was their adored only son who could do no wrong in their eyes—and then he had the advantage of being away at school. Luckily, perhaps, their favourites were not always the same. For my father there would be one child who was allowed every licence and one who was getting what we used to call rat week—the rest of us floated in a sort of limbo between these two extremes. The change would come with dramatic suddenness and for no apparent reason. Of course, one kept a weather eye open for it, but even after years of experience nobody could prophesy when it would occur or what direction it would take. My mother, who was not violent like my father, never seemed, as he often did, actively to loathe any of us. She was entirely influenced by physical beauty; those who were passing through an awkward or ugly age were less in favour than their prettier sisters.

Blor, however, must have been superhuman; she seemed to have no favourites at all. If she felt on the side of the little ones, especially her own baby, Diana, against the bully that I was, she never showed it. Her fairness always amazed me, even as a child. My vile behaviour to the others was partly, I suppose, the result of jealousy and partly of a longing to be grown up and live with grown-up people. The others bored me, and I made them feel it. They banded together against me; my mother still has a badge carefully embroidered with 'Leag against Nancy, hed Tom'. I expect I would have been much worse but for Blor. My mother's scoldings and my father's whippings had little effect, but Blor at least made me feel ashamed of myself. Of course, I ought to have gone to school—it was the dream of my life—but there was never any question of that.

Diana thinks that the one Blor really preferred was Decca. 'Hurry up, Jessica—stop dawdling.' She was a dawdler if ever there was one. 'Put those shoes on, Jessica. Whatever are you doing?' 'I love yer, m'Hinket' (her own name for Blor). Personally, I thought it was Debo. But I believe there was very little in it; she loved us all.

Long after we were grown up she went back to Egham to live with her brother and sister. She died at a great age, nearly ninety.

Useless to pretend that the Nanny in *The Blessing* is not based on Blor. She has all her mannerisms and many of her prejudices, but she is a caricature. When I sent Blor the book I said: 'This is a story about a Nanny very much unlike you, darling.' She wrote back; '. . . I felt quite sorry for the poor Nanny—all that packing!' I have written this about her to try and present her as she really was.

1962

A Bad Time

APSLEY CHERRY GARRARD has said that 'polar explora-
tion is at once the cleanest and most isolated way of having
a bad time that has yet been devised'.[1] Nobody could deny
that he and the twenty-four other members of Captain
Scott's expedition to the South Pole had a bad time; in fact,
all other bad times, embarked on by men of their own free
will, pale before it. Theirs is the last of the great classic
explorations; their equipment, though they lived in our
century, curiously little different from that used by Captain
Cook. Vitamin pills would probably have saved the lives of
the Polar party, so would a wireless transmitter; an electric
torch have mitigated the misery of the Winter Journey.
How many things which we take completely as a matter of
course had not yet been invented, such a little time ago!
Scott's *Terra Nova* had the advantage over Cook's *Resolu-
tion* of steam as well as sail. Even this was a mixed blessing,
as it involved much hateful shovelling, while the coal occupied space which could have been put to better account in
the little wooden barque (764 tons). Three motor-sledges
lashed to the deck seemed marvellously up-to-date and were
the pride and joy of Captain Scott.

The *Terra Nova* sailed from London 15th June 1910

[1] Unless otherwise stated, the quotations in this essay are from
The Worst Journey in the World, by Cherry Garrard.

16

and from New Zealand 26th November. She was fearfully overloaded; on deck, as well as the motor-sledges in their huge crates, there were 30 tons of coal in sacks, $2\frac{1}{2}$ tons of petrol in drums, 33 dogs, and 19 ponies. She rode out a bad storm by a miracle. 'Bowers and Campbell were standing upon the bridge and the ship rolled sluggishly over until the lee combings of the main hatch were under the sea . . . as a rule, if a ship goes that far over she goes down.' It took her thirty-eight days to get to McMurdo Sound, by which time the men were in poor shape. They had slept in their clothes, lucky if they got five hours a night, and had had no proper meals. As soon as they dropped anchor they began to unload the ship. This entailed dragging its cargo over ice floes which were in constant danger of being tipped up by killer whales, a very tricky business, specially when it came to moving ponies, motor sledges and a pianola. Then they built the Hut which was henceforward to be their home. Scott, tireless himself, always drove his men hard and these things were accomplished in a fortnight. The *Terra Nova* sailed away; she was to return the following summer, when it was hoped that the Polar party would be back in time to be taken off before the freezing up of the sea forced her to leave again. If not, they would be obliged to spend a second winter on McMurdo Sound. Winter, of course, in those latitudes, happens during our summer months and is perpetual night, as the summer is perpetual day. The stunning beauty of the scenery affected the men deeply. When the sun shone the snow was never white, but brilliant shades of pink, blue and lilac; in winter the aurora australis flamed across the sky and the summit of Mount Erebus glowed.

The Hut, unlike so much of Scott's equipment, was a

total success. It was built on the shore, too near the sea, perhaps, for absolute security in the cruel winter storms, under the active volcano Mount Erebus, called after the ship in which Ross discovered these regions in 1839. It was 50 feet by 25, 9 feet high. The walls had double boarding inside and outside the frames, with layers of quilted seaweed between the boards. The roof had six layers of alternate wood, rubber and seaweed. Though 109 degrees of frost was quite usual, the men never suffered from cold indoors; in fact, with twenty-five of them living there, the cooking range at full blast and a stove at the other end, they sometimes complained of stuffiness.

Life during the first winter was very pleasant. Before turning in for good they had done several gruelling marches, laying stores in depots along the route of the Polar journey; they felt they needed and had earned a rest. Their only complaint was that there were too many lectures; Scott insisted on at least three a week and they seem to have bored the others considerably—except for Ponting's magic lantern slides of Japan. A gramophone and a pianola provided background music and there was a constant flow of witticisms which one assumes to have been unprintable until one learns that Dr Wilson would leave the company if a coarse word were spoken. In the Hut they chiefly lived on flesh of seals, which they killed without difficulty, since these creatures are friendly and trustful by nature. 'A sizzling on the fire and a smell of porridge and seal liver heralded breakfast which was at 8 a.m. in theory and a good deal later in practice.' Supper was at 7. Most were in their bunks by 10 p.m., sometimes with a candle and a book; the acetylene was turned off at 10.30 to economize the fuel. Cherry Garrard tells us that the talk at meals was never

dull. Most of these men were from the Royal Navy, and
sailors are often droll, entertaining fellows possessing much
out-of-the-way information. (Nobody who heard them can
have forgotten the performances of Commander Campbell
on the B.B.C.—he was one of the greatest stars they ever
had, in my view.) Heated arguments would break out on a
diversity of subjects, to be settled by recourse to an encyclo-
pedia or an atlas or sometimes a Latin dictionary. They
wished they had also brought a *Who's Who*. One of their
discussions, which often recurred, concerned 'Why are we
here? What is the force that drives us to undergo severe,
sometimes ghastly hardships of our own free will?' The
reply was The Interests of Science—it is important that man
should know the features of the world he lives in, but this
was not a complete answer. Once there was a discussion as
to whether they would continue to like Polar travel if, by the
aid of modern inventions, it became quite easy amd comfortable. They said no, with one accord. It seems as if they
really wanted to prove to themselves how much they could
endure. Their rewards were a deep spiritual satisfaction
and relationships between men who had become more than
brothers.

Their loyalty to each other was fantastic—there was
no jealousy, bickering, bullying or unkindness. Reading
between the lines of their diaries and records it is impossible to guess whether anybody disliked anybody
else. As for The Owner, as they called Scott, they all
worshipped and blindly followed him. Cherry Garrard, the
only one who could be called an intellectual and who took a
fairly objective view of the others, gives an interesting
account of Scott's character: subtle, he says, full of light and
shade. No sense of humour—peevish by nature, highly

strung, irritable, melancholy and moody. However, such was his strength of mind that he overcame these faults, though he could not entirely conceal long periods of sadness. He was humane, so fond of animals that he refused to take dogs on long journeys, hauling the sledge himself rather than see them suffer. His idealism and intense patriotism shone through all he wrote. Of course, he had the extraordinary charm without which no man can be a leader. In his diaries he appears as an affectionate person, but shyness or the necessary isolation of a sea-captain prevented him from showing this side to the others. He was poor; he worried about provision for his family when it became obvious that he would never return to them. Indeed, he was always hampered by lack of money and never had enough to finance his voyages properly. Lady Kennet, his widow, once told me that Scott only took on Cherry Garrard because he subscribed £2,000 to the expedition. He thought him too young (23), too delicate and too short-sighted, besides being quite inexperienced; he was the only amateur in the party. It is strange and disgraceful that Scott, who was already a world-famous explorer, should have had so little support from the Government for this prestigious voyage.

These men had an enemy, not with them in the Hut but ever present in their minds. His shadow fell across their path before they left New Zealand, when Captain Scott received a telegram dated from Madeira, with the laconic message *Am going South Amundsen*. Now, Amundsen was known to be preparing Nansen's old ship, the *Fram*, for a journey, having announced that he intended to do some further exploring in the Arctic. Only when he was actually at sea did he tell his crew that he was on his way to try and reach the South Pole. There seemed something underhand

and unfair about this. Scott's men were furious; they talked of finding the Amundsen party and having it out with them, but Scott put a good face on it and pretended not to mind at all. The two leaders could hardly have been more different. Amundsen was cleverer than Scott, 'an explorer of a markedly intellectual type rather Jewish than Scandinavian'. There was not much humanity or idealism about him, he was a tough, brave professional. He had a sense of humour and his description of flying over the North Pole in a dirigible with General Nobile is very funny indeed. Nobile was for ever in tears and Amundsen on the verge of striking him, the climax coming when, over the Pole, Nobile threw out armfuls of huge Italian flags which caught in the propeller and endangered their lives. All the same, Amundsen died going to the rescue of Nobile in 1928.

No doubt the knowledge that 'the Norskies' were also on their way to the Pole was a nagging worry to Scott all those long, dark, winter months, though he was very careful to hide his feelings and often remarked that Amundsen had a perfect right to go anywhere at any time. 'The Pole is not a race,' he would say. He (Scott) was going in the interests of science and not in order to 'get there first'. But he knew that everybody else would look on it as a race; he was only human, he longed to win it.

The chief of Scott's scientific staff and his greatest friend was Dr Wilson. He was to Scott what Sir Joseph Hooker had been to Ross. (Incredible as it seems, Hooker only died that very year, 1911. Scott knew him well.) Wilson was a doctor of St George's Hospital and a zoologist specializing in vertebrates. He had published a book on whales, penguins and seals and had prepared a report for the Royal Commission on grouse disease. While he was

doing this Cherry Garrard met him, at a shooting lodge in
Scotland, and became fired with a longing to go south.
Wilson was an accomplished water-colourist. Above all, he
was an adorable person: 'The finest character I ever met,'
said Scott. Now Dr Wilson wanted to bring home the egg of
an Emperor Penguin. He had studied these huge
creatures when he was with Scott on his first journey to
the Antarctic and thought that their embryos would be of
paramount biological interest, possibly proving to be the
missing link between bird and fish. The Emperors, who
weigh 6½ stone, look like sad little men and were often
taken by early explorers for human natives of the South
Polar regions, are in a low state of evolution (and of spirits).
They lay their eggs in the terrible mid-winter, because
only thus can their chicks, which develop with a slowness
abnormal in birds, be ready to survive the next winter. They
never step on shore, even to breed; they live in rookeries
on sea-ice. To incubate their eggs, they balance them on
their enormous feet and press them against a patch of bare
skin on the abdomen protected from the cold by a lappet of
skin and feathers. Paternity is the only joy known to these
wretched birds and a monstrous instinct for it is implanted
in their breasts; male and female hatch out the eggs and
nurse the chicks, also on their feet, indiscriminately. When
a penguin has to go in the sea to catch his dinner he leaves
egg or chick on the ice; there is then a mad scuffle as twenty
childless birds rush to adopt it, quite often breaking or
killing it in the process. They will nurse a dead chick until
it falls to pieces and sit for months on an addled egg or even
a stone. All this happens in darkness and about a hundred
degrees of frost. I often think the R.S.P.C.A. ought to do
something for the Emperor Penguins.

A Bad Time

Dr Wilson had reason to suppose that there was a rookery of Emperors at Cape Crozier, about sixty miles along the coast. When the ghastly winter weather had properly set in he asked for two volunteers to go with him and collect some eggs. It was one of the rules in the Hut that everybody volunteered for everything, so Wilson really chose his own companions: 'Birdie' Bowers, considered by Scott to be the hardest traveller in the world, and Cherry Garrard. The three of them left the light and warmth and good cheer of the Hut to embark upon the most appalling nightmare possible to imagine. The darkness was profound and invariable. (They steered by Jupiter.) The temperature was generally in the region of 90 degrees of frost, unless there was a blizzard, when it would rise as high as 40 degrees of frost, producing other forms of discomfort and the impossibility of moving. The human body exudes a quantity of sweat and moisture, even in the lowest temperatures, so the men's clothes were soon frozen as stiff as boards and they were condemned to remain in the bending position in which they pulled their sleigh. It was as though they were dressed in lead. The surface of the snow was so bad that they had to divide their load and bring it along by relays. They could never take off their huge gloves for fear of losing their hands by frostbite; as it was, their fingers were covered with blisters in which the liquid was always frozen, so that their hands were like bunches of marbles. The difficulty of performing the simplest action with them may be imagined; it sometimes took over an hour to light a match and as much as nine hours to pitch their tent and do the work of the camp. Everything was slow, slow. When they had a discussion it lasted a week. If Cherry Garrard had written his book in a more uninhibited age he would no doubt have told us how they managed about what the Americans call going to the bathroom.[1] As it is, this interesting point remains mysterious. Dr Wilson insisted on them spending seven hours out of the twenty-four (day and night in that total blackness were quite arbitrary) in their sleeping-bags. These were always frozen up, so that it took at least an hour to worm their way in and then they suffered the worst of all the tortures. Normally on such journeys the great comfort was sleep. Once in their warm dry sleeping-bags the men went off as if they were drugged and nothing, neither pain nor worry, could keep them awake. But now the cold was too intense for Wilson and Cherry Garrard to close an eye. They lay shivering until they thought their backs would break, enviously listening to the regular snores of Birdie. They had got a spirit lamp—the only bearable moments they knew were when they had just swallowed a hot drink; for a little while it was like a hot-water bottle on their hearts; but the effect soon wore off. Their teeth froze and split to pieces. Their toe-nails came away. Cherry Garrard began to long for death. It never occurred to any of them to go back. The penguin's egg assumed such importance in their minds, as they groped and plodded their four or five miles a day, that the whole future of the human race might have depended on their finding one.

At last, in the bleakest and most dreadful place imaginable, they heard the Emperors calling. To get to the rookery entailed a long, dangerous feat of mountaineering, since it was at the foot of an immense cliff. Dim twilight now glowed for an hour or two at midday, so they were able to

[1]'They [the savages] go to the bathroom in the street.' (Report from a member of the Peace Corps in the Congo).

see the birds, about a hundred of them, mournfully huddled together, trying to shuffle away from the intruders without losing the eggs from their feet and trumpeting with curious metallic voices. The men took some eggs, got lost on the cliff, were nearly killed several times by falling into crevasses and broke all the eggs but two. That night there was a hurricane and their tent blew away, carried out to sea, no doubt. Now that they faced certain death, life suddenly seemed more attractive. They lay in their sleeping-bags for two days waiting for the wind to abate and pretending to each other that they would manage somehow to get home without a tent, although they knew very well that they must perish. When it was possible to move again Bowers, by a miracle, found the tent. 'We were so thankful we said nothing.' They could hardly remember the journey home— it passed like a dreadful dream, and indeed they often slept while pulling their sleigh. When they arrived, moribund, at the Hut, exactly one month after setting forth, The Owner said: 'Look here, you know, this is the hardest journey that has ever been done.'

I once recounted this story to a hypochondriac friend, who said, horrified, 'But it must have been so *bad* for them.' The extraordinary thing is that it did them no harm. They were quite recovered three months later, in time for the Polar journey, from which, of course, Wilson and Bowers did not return, but which they endured longer than any except Scott himself. Cherry Garrard did most of the Polar journey; he went through the 1914 war, in the trenches much of the time, and lived until 1959.

As for the penguins' eggs, when Cherry Garrard got back to London the first thing he did was to take them to the Natural History Museum. Alas, nobody was very much

interested in them. The Chief Custodian, when he received
Cherry Garrard after a good long delay, simply put them
down on an ink stand and went on talking to a friend.
Cherry Garrard asked if he could have a receipt for the
eggs? 'It's not necessary. It's all right. You needn't wait,'
he was told.

The Winter Journey was so appalling that the journey to
the Pole, which took place in daylight and in much higher
temperatures seemed almost banal by comparison; but it
was terribly long (over seven hundred miles each way) and
often very hard. Scott left the Hut at 11 p.m. on 1st
November. He soon went back, for a book; was undecided
what to take, but finally chose a volume of Browning. He
was accompanied by a party of about twenty men with two
motor-sledges (the third had fallen into the sea while being
landed), ponies and dogs. Only four men were to go to the
Pole, but they were to be accompanied until the dreaded
Beardmore glacier had been climbed. The men in charge
of the motors turned back first, the motors having proved a
failure. They delayed the party with continual breakdowns
and only covered fifty miles. The dogs and their drivers
went next. The ponies were shot at the foot of the glacier.
The men minded this; they had become attached to the
beasts, who had done their best, often in dreadful conditions. So far the journey had taken longer than it should
have. The weather was bad for travelling, too warm, the
snow too soft; there were constant blizzards. Now they
were twelve men, without ponies or dogs, manhauling the
sledges. As they laboured up the Beardmore, Scott was
choosing the men who would go to the Pole with him.
Of course, the disappointment of those who were sent home

at this stage was acute; they had done most of the gruelling journey and were not to share in the glory. On 20th December Cherry Garrard wrote: 'This evening has been rather a shock. As I was getting my finesko on to the top of my ski Scott came up to me and said he had rather a blow for me. Of course, I knew what he was going to say, but could hardly grasp that I was going back—tomorrow night. . . . Wilson told me it was a toss-up whether Titus [Oates] or I should go on; that being so I think Titus will help him more than I can. I said all I could think of—he seemed so cut up about it, saying "I think somehow it is specially hard on you." I said I hoped I had not disappointed him and he caught hold of me and said "No, no—no", so if that is the case all is well.'

There was still one more party left to be sent back after Cherry Garrard's. Scott said in his diary: 'I dreaded this necessity of choosing, nothing could be more heartrending.' He added: 'We are struggling on, considering all things against odds. The weather is a constant anxiety.' The weather was against them; the winter which succeeded this disappointing summer set in early and was the worst which hardened Arctic travellers had ever experienced.

Scott had always intended to take a party of four to the Pole. He now made the fatal decision to take five. Oates was the last-minute choice; it is thought that Scott felt the Army ought to be represented. So they were: Scott aged 43, Wilson 39, Seaman Evans 37, Bowers 28, and Oates 32. The extra man was *de trop* in every way. There were only four pairs of skis; the tent was too small for five, so that one man was too near the outside and always cold; worst of all, there were now five people to eat rations meant for four. It was an amazing mistake, but it showed that Scott thought

27

he was on a good wicket. The returning parties certainly thought so; it never occurred to them that he would have much difficulty, let alone that his life might be in danger. But they were all more exhausted than they knew and the last two parties only got home by the skin of their teeth, after hair-raising experiences on the Beardmore. Scott still had 150 miles to go.

On 16th January, only a few miles from the Pole, Bowers spied something in the snow—an abandoned sledge. Then they came upon dog tracks. Man Friday's footsteps on the sand were less dramatic. They knew that the enemy had won. 'The Norwegians have forestalled us,' wrote Scott, 'and are first at the Pole. . . . All the day dreams must go; it will be a wearisome return'. And he wrote at the Pole itself: 'Great God! This is an awful place!'

Amundsen had left his base on 20th October with three other men, all on skis, and sixty underfed dogs to pull his sleighs. He went over the Axel Herberg glacier, an easier climb than the Beardmore, and reached the Pole on 16th December with no more discomfort than on an ordinary Antarctic journey. His return only took thirty-eight days, by which time he had eaten most of the dogs, beginning with his own favourite. When the whole story was known there was a good deal of feeling in England over these animals. At the Royal Geographical Society's dinner to Amundsen the President, Lord Curzon, infuriated his guest by ending his speech with the words, 'I think we ought to give three cheers for the dogs.'

And now for the long pull home. Evans was dying, of frostbite and concussion from a fall. He never complained, just staggered along, sometimes wandering in his mind. The relief when he died was tremendous, as Scott had been tormented by feeling that perhaps he ought to abandon him, for the sake of the others. When planning the Winter Journey, Wilson had told Cherry Garrard that he was against taking seamen on the toughest ventures—he said they simply would not look after themselves. Indeed, Evans had concealed a wound on his hand which was the beginning of his troubles. A month later, the party was again delayed, by Oates's illness; he was in terrible pain from frostbitten feet. He bravely committed suicide, but too late to save the others. Scott wrote: 'Oates' last thoughts were of his mother, but immediately before he took pride in thinking that his regiment would be pleased at the bold way in which he met his death. . . . He was a brave soul. He slept through the night, hoping not to wake; but he woke in the morning, yesterday. It was blowing a blizzard. He said "I am just going outside and may be some time." '

All, now, were ill. Their food was short and the petrol for their spirit lamp, left for them in the depots, had mostly evaporated. The horrible pemmican, with its low vitamin content, which was their staple diet was only bearable when made into a hot stew. Now they were eating it cold, keeping the little fuel they had to make hot cocoa. (This business of the petrol was very hard on the survivors. When on their way home, the returning parties had made use of it, carefully taking much less than they were told was their share. They always felt that Scott, who never realized that it had evaporated, must have blamed them in his heart for the shortage.) Now the weather changed. 'They were in evil case but they would have been all right if the cold had not come down upon them; unexpected, unforetold and fatal. The cold in itself was not so tremendous until you realize that they had been out four months, that they had fought their way up the biggest glacier in the world, in feet of soft snow, that they had spent seven weeks under plateau conditions of rarified air, big winds and low temperatures.' They struggled on and might just have succeeded in getting home if they had had ordinary good luck. But, eleven miles from the depot which would have saved them, a blizzard blew up so that they could not move. It blew for a week, at the end of which there was no more hope. On 29th March Scott wrote: 'My dear Mrs Wilson. If this reaches you, Bill and I will have gone out together. We are very near it now and I should like you to know how splendid he was at the end—everlastingly cheerful and ready to sacrifice himself for others, never a word of blame to me for leading him into this mess. He is suffering, luckily, only minor discomforts.

His eyes have a comfortable blue look of hope and his mind is peaceful with the satisfaction of his faith, in regarding himself as part of the great scheme of the Almighty. I can do no more to comfort you than to tell you that he died, as he lived, a brave, true man—the best of comrades and staunchest of friends. My whole heart goes out to you in pity.

Yours R. Scott.'

And to Sir James Barrie:

'We are pegging out in a very comfortless spot . . . I am not at all afraid of the end but sad to miss many a humble pleasure which I had planned for the future on our long marches. . . . We have had four days of storm in our tent and nowhere's food or fuel. We did intend to finish ourselves when things proved like this but we have decided to die naturally in the track.'

On 19th March Cherry Garrard and the others in the

Hut, none of them fit, began to be worried. The *Terra Nova* had duly come back, with longed-for mails and news of the outer world. They had to let her go again, taking those who were really ill. On 27th March Atkinson, the officer in charge, and a seaman went a little way to try and meet the Polar party, but it was a hopeless quest, and they were 100 miles from where Scott was already dead when they turned back. They now prepared for another winter in the Hut, the sadness of which can be imagined. Long, long after they knew all hope was gone they used to think they heard their friends coming in, or saw shadowy forms that seemed to be theirs. They mourned them and missed their company. Scott, Wilson and Bowers had been the most dynamic of them all, while 'Titus' or 'Farmer Hayseed' (Oates) was a dear, good-natured fellow whom everybody loved to tease. The weather was unimaginably awful. It seemed impossible that the Hut could stand up to the tempests which raged outside for weeks on end and the men quite expected that it might collapse at any time. When at last the sun reappeared they set forth to see if they could discover traces of their friends. They hardly expected any results, as they were firmly convinced that the men must have fallen down a crevasse on the Beardmore, a fate they had all escaped by inches at one time or another. Terribly soon, however, they came upon what looked like a cairn; it was, in fact, Scott's tent covered with snow.

'We have found them. To say it has been a ghastly day cannot express it. Bowers and Wilson were sleeping in their bags. Scott had thrown the flaps of his bag open at the end. His left hand was stretched over Wilson, his lifelong friend.' Everything was tidy, their papers and records in perfect order. Atkinson and Cherry Garrard read enough to find out what had happened and packed up the rest of the papers unopened. They built a cairn over the tent, which was left as they found it. Near the place where Oates disappeared they put up a cross with the inscription: 'Hereabouts died a very gallant gentleman, Captain E. G. Oates of the Inniskilling Dragoons. In March 1912, returning from the Pole, he walked willingly to his death in a blizzard to try and save his comrades, beset by hardship.'

In due course Cherry Garrard and the others were taken off by the *Terra Nova*. When they arrived in New Zealand Atkinson went ashore to send cables to the dead men's wives. 'The Harbour Master came out in the tug with him. "Come down here a minute," said Atkinson to me and "It's made a tremendous impression. I had no idea it would make so much," he said.' Indeed it had. The present writer well remembers this impression, though only seven at the time.

Amundsen had won the race, but Scott had captured his fellow countrymen's imagination. It is one of our endearing qualities, perhaps unique, that we think no less of a man because he has failed—we even like him better for it. In any case, Amundsen complained that a year later a Norwegian boy at school in England was being taught that Captain Scott discovered the South Pole.

I don't quite know why I have felt the need to write down this well-known story, making myself cry twice, at the inscription on Oates's cross and when Atkinson said, 'It has made a tremendous impression.' Perhaps the bold, bald men who get, smiling, into cupboards, as if they were playing sardines, go a little way (about as far as from London to Manchester) into the air and come out of their cupboards again, a few hours later, smiling more than ever, have put me in mind of other adventurers. It is fifty years to the day, as I write this, that Scott died. Most of the wonderful books which tell of his expedition are out of print now, but they can easily be got at second hand. I should like to feel that I may have induced somebody to read them again.

Books relating to the Polar journey: *Scott's Last Expedition;* Cherry-Garrard: *The Worst Journey in the World;* Priestly: *Antarctic Adventure;* E. R. Evans: *South with Scott;* Amundsen: *My Life as an Explorer.*

1962

Augustus Hare, 1834–1903

Memorials of a Quiet Life, in three volumes. *The Story of Two Noble Lives,* in three volumes. *The Story of My Life,* in six volumes. *Walks in Rome. Days Near Paris. Cities of Northern Italy.* And so on. A dream of croquet parties on rectory lawns, of amiable peeresses, of cypress and myrtle and evening bells across the water meadows. Born to financial independence, into a highly cultivated society, with leisure and not without talent, who would not now change places with Augustus Hare? If a glance at his photograph reveals the face of a sulky badger, there is compensation lower down; the waistcoat, the watch chain are tightly stretched over dairy produce and fine wines—oh to have been Augustus Hare.[1] Escape, then, into this dream as it rambles on, volume after volume, but turning, as dreams do, into something liverish and unpleasant, with sinister undercurrents and sensations so disagreeable, so much like a nightmare, that it is finally an extreme relief to wake up and realize that face, figure and fortune are after all not those of Augustus Hare.

In 1834 a son was born in Rome to the Francis Hares, an attractive, feckless couple who were displeased at the birth of another child, their fourth. They named him after a clergyman brother of his father's who had died in Rome only

[1] This essay was written in wartime.

a few weeks previously and whose last (written) words had been 'Oh, Lady Blessington, if you knew how much I wish I could hope I was sure of meeting you in the place to which God is taking me.' The childless widow of this brother presently wrote and asked Mrs Francis Hare whether she could adopt the young Augustus. The reply was startling— 'Yes, certainly, the baby shall be sent as soon as it is weaned, and if anybody else would like one would you kindly recollect that we have others.' At the age of fourteen months the child was duly dispatched to England, with two nightshirts and a coral necklace, rather as a puppy might be sent complete with collar and chain; henceforward his own parents assumed the relationship of a singularly unaffectionate aunt and uncle, while Mrs Augustus Hare became, in all but fact, his mother. That she loved him from the first moment there is no doubt; his love for her was exaggerated. All should have been perfect happiness. Unfortunately, however, she had chosen to settle at Lime House, near Hurstmonceux, where her brother-in-law, Julius Hare, was rector, and she fell utterly and completely under his influence.

Julius Hare seems to have been well enough liked by his own contemporaries; such men as Walter Savage Landor, John Sterling, Arthur Stanley and Dr Arnold regarded him as a particularly urbane and enlightened character. Perhaps he was in love with Mrs Augustus Hare (he dined at her house every evening) and jealous of the child; perhaps he honestly believed that Christian cruelty ought to be practised on the young; in any case towards Augustus he was a veritable Mr Murdstone. From the age of five there were continual executions with a riding-whip on the poor child, who when Uncle Julius

arrived would be sent upstairs to 'prepare'—he knew only
too well what for. Huge doses of rhubarb and senna were
administered with a view to teaching him that carnal
indulgences must be avoided; delicious puddings were
placed before him at dinner which he was made to carry,
untasted, to some poor family. Much worse, however, was
in store. When Augustus was nine and had been for some
months at his horrible first school he went with Mrs Hare
and Uncle Julius for a tour in the Lake District. Mrs Hare
had invited a schoolteacher called Esther Maurice to join
the party, 'never foreseeing, what everyone else foresaw,
that Uncle Julius, who always had a passion for governesses,
would certainly propose to her. Bitter were the tears my
mother shed when this . . . actually took place. It was the most
dismal of betrothals. Esther sobbed and cried, my mother
sobbed and cried, Uncle Julius sobbed and cried daily.'

If Julius Hare was Mr Murdstone, his new wife was to
the very life Miss Murdstone. Uncle Julius, of course,
dined no more at Lime House, but Aunt Esther, who
evidently had a talent for creating miserable situations,
insisted that Mrs Hare and Augustus should dine every
evening at the rectory and that in winter they should stay
the night, going home before breakfast in the morning.

Augustus was always left alone in a dark, unheated room
until dinner-time. At dinner he was discouraged from
speaking; if he did venture a remark it was received with
withering sarcasm. His bed was a straw palliasse and
a single blanket; in spite of the fact that the chilblains on
his hands and feet were open sores, he was never allowed
warm water for washing; he often had to break the ice with
a candlestick. On Sundays his mother gave in to a suggestion
of Aunt Esther's that he should be locked into the vestry of

the church between services. 'Open war was declared at length between Aunt Esther and myself. I had a favourite cat called Selma which I adored. Aunt Esther saw this and insisted that the cat must be given up to her. I wept over it in agonies of grief, but Aunt Esther insisted. . . . For some time it comforted me for going to the rectory because then I possibly saw my idolized Selma. But soon there came a day when Selma was missing: Aunt Esther had ordered her to be hung.'

The mother, as Augustus calls Mrs Hare, instead of being appalled by their cruelties, fell more and more under the influence of these devil worshippers. She conceived it her duty to withhold any manifestations of sympathy from the poor little boy. When he came home for the holidays, ready to throw himself into her arms, she never went to the hall to meet him, and he speaks of 'the awful chill of going into the drawing-room and seeing my longed and pined for mother sit still in her chair by the fire'. He was sent to a series of schools where he was starved and beaten, but taught nothing. His back was supposed to be weak and he went to Harrow wearing a kind of harness which saved him from 'things which never could be mentioned but which were of nightly occurrence all over the school', but did not strengthen his constitution. He seems to have been an unattractive boy, neither schoolmates, cousins, aunts nor uncles liked him much; the only person to show him any kindness or human sympathy during the whole of his childhood was old Walter Savage Landor.

This odious upbringing produced a pathetic but odious personality, a prig, a snob, touchy and irritable. 'Augustus Hare was a tedious toady,' said my grandfather. He seems to have eschewed youth and to have been afraid of his own contemporaries, contact with whom he avoided through his morbid attachment to 'the mother'. With a devotion worthy of a better cause he hardly ever left her side. As soon as he was grown up they travelled about Europe together for months at a time. During these journeys Hare began to accumulate the mass of information which finally went into his famous guide-books. Unlike the modern tourist, mother and son took the trouble to enter into the life of the various places they visited and to make friends with the inhabitants. He described some of these in a way their descendants may find rather displeasing. 'The Duchess of Sermonetta—a most ghastly and solemn woman to outsiders.' 'Princess Borghese, by birth Adèle de La Rochefoucauld, had the reputation of having poisoned the beautiful Princess Gwendolina.'

Finally he nursed 'the mother' through an interminable illness and a series of death-bed scenes which spread over several years. They occupy a whole volume of his own autobiography as well as a substantial part of the *Memorials of a Quiet Life*. Quiet though the rest of her life may have been, her last months were, in fact, most exciting. She developed an unmanageable arm, which began by stealing her pocket handkerchiefs, but soon threw itself upon her person, strangling and buffeting her and otherwise giving an excellent imitation of an all-in wrestling match. Augustus did his best to defend her, but it was uphill work, and when at last the K.O. had been delivered he found himself, at 36, quite worn out by his dual role of sick nurse and referee. He retired for many months to Holmwood, the country house which 'the mother' had left him, and wrote her *Memorials*.

From now on Hare was perfectly free to indulge in his two hobbies, the aristocracy and the supernatural. The emotional blank left in his life by the loss of 'the mother' was filled by Lady Waterford, and he was soon installed at Highcliffe Castle as daughter of the house. Lord Waterford, of course, would not have tolerated him for a moment, but then poor Lord Waterford's body had been brought home from hunting, on a gate, some years before.

Lady Waterford having both her arms under perfect control, this relationship was less exacting than that with 'the mother'; it left him with plenty of time and energy to dine out, pay country-house visits and collect his ghost stories. They are written down at length in *The Story of My Life* and fall roughly into two categories: the figure from the dead who appears in order to warn some high-born lady that her mad butler is approaching with an axe, or that the train she is sitting in will shortly be derailed (mad butlers and railway accidents seem to have been the ever-present dangers of those days), and the heap of human bones in the best spare room which nightly nags at the guests until the aristocratic host is prevailed upon to give it Christian burial. In short they are both dull and improbable; soon, when reading the *Life*, one's eye learns that paragraphs which open 'Some years ago there was a young lady living in Ireland. . . .' or 'Lord So and So often used to tell how . . .' are to be skipped. Very fascinating, however, is the light thrown on the medical history of the age. It is perhaps hardly surprising that Georgiana Hare-Naylor, who undertook to dance the clock round at Bonn, should have had to lie on her back for a year after performing this feat, but what are we to make of Edward Liddell, cured of typhoid by lying under a vast poultice of snow, of Aunt Caroline who ate one of her maid's arms and part of another, or of Mrs Hare-Naylor who wore out her optic nerve by painting too many water-colours of Hurstmonceux Castle, went blind and died in great agony? Priscilla Maurice, sister of Aunt Esther and authoress of *Sickness, its Trials and Blessings*, was violently sick after everything she ate for many years. Sarah Hare died from eating ices when over-heated at a ball. There was also the savage, paralytic Mr Dashwood—surely a contradiction in terms? The case of Esmeralda Hare, the romantic, beautiful sister of Augustus, is the oddest of all. When a small child she swallowed a wooden thimble with a copper band; the thimble dissolved with time, the copper band remained in her body, growing as she grew until attenuated to the minutest thread. She was warned by the doctors that she must avoid a damp climate and eschew vegetables. In vain. She died, not very young it is true, but not in the fullness of age, and her horrible symptoms were those of verdigris poisoning. Augustus was a fervent amateur of death-beds; he rushed to attend them upon the smallest excuse or greedily garnered up details from those who had. A great deal of dying seems to have taken place on graves; dogs and cats die on each other's and on their master's graves, and Aunt Esther died after lying for hours on Uncle Julius's in the pouring rain.

'I went alone with the Duke to the kitchen garden and to the fine stables where there are still sixty horses.' So the *Life* goes on, tittle tattle, tittle tattle, volume after volume. Never a mention of politics, nothing very profound on art or literature. 'Raeburn's paintings may be slight . . . but his men never fail to be gentlemen and his women are always ladies.' When Hare's book about the Marchioness of Waterford and Countess Canning came out he remarks, 'My *Story of Two Noble Lives* appeared and was warmly

'. . . to warn some high-born lady that her mad butler is approaching
with an axe.'

welcomed by the upper classes of Society, for whom it was especially written.' There can hardly have been a country house of importance which he did not visit, hardly an aristocratic family whose praises, especially exaggerated in the case of sweet-faced old dowagers, he does not sing. 'Dear Lady Ruthven is stone deaf, almost blind and her voice is like wagon wheels, but in her 86th year she is as kind and good and truly witty as ever.' More and more he identifies high rank with saintliness, noble birth with noble lives and even the phenomena of nature with the landed classes. 'The Earth has already perished once . . . and there are geological features, especially at Lord Lansdowne's place in Ireland, which prove it.' And yet the man was not a fool, his guide-books show a high degree of learning, are classics in their way and, in spite of the gulf between his taste and ours, still extremely readable. In fact, the *Walks in London*, packed as it is with information about so much of London that has recently been destroyed, more alas, by its own citizens than by the Germans, should prove an invaluable record to future generations. Even here, however, it is too easy to perceive his besetting weakness. The Wallace Collection, he says, 'allows the public to see in perfection art treasures which so frequently decorate the homes of the English nobility'. At Grosvenor House, where the noble collection can only be seen by personal application to the Duke, and where the treasures are displayed in pleasant rooms used by the family, he is greatly impressed by 'the haughty, expressive statue of Marie Antoinette on her way to execution, by Lord Ronald Gower'. Belgravia is 'this eerily ugly part of London, wholly devoid of interest, where none would think of visiting unless drawn thither by the claims of Society'.

What had 'the mother', Aunt Esther and Uncle Julius done to turn a sad, affectionate, clever little boy into such a tremendous snob? Towards the end his book is saturated in self-pity. His intimate friends were all dead, which is only natural, as they were old enough to have been his great-aunts; the boys he befriended (he had a curious little home life very much centred on the befriending of boys) had all gone to the bad. There was nobody left with whom he could share his memories of departed and departing gentry, there would be nobody to tend his death-bed. Poor Augustus Hare. In spite of the peace, the leisure and the security of his era, in spite of the high vitamin content of his diet, his had not been a very happy or enviable existence. 'Base men', he says, 'avoid me.' One can't help seeing why.

1942

Reading for Pleasure

As far as I am concerned, all reading is for pleasure. My eyesight is erratic and when I am bored by a book physical agony soon compels me to put it down. On the other hand, if I am interested and amused I can go on for quite a long time. Of course, this has not always been so. I cannot remember not being able to read and as a child I lived in books; my most vivid early recollections come from them. Public events such as the outbreak of war or the murder of the Romanovs made more impression on me than family ones, because they were part of that fascinating serial called History. I read quickly and guiltily. Reading was tolerated but not at all encouraged by my father, who thought it a waste of time. 'If you've got nothing to do', he would say, finding one with a book, 'run down to the village and tell Hooper . . .'

There were certain very strict rules, continually broken. Reading in bed and in the bath were forbidden; novels not allowed before luncheon; library books to be read in the library only. By good luck all my forebears except my father were literate and our house was full of books—classics in the library and the usual (excellent) children's books of the day in the schoolroom, left there by my aunts, the youngest of whom was only eight years older than me. Though my father never read himself, he had learnt from his father to respect a volume as an object, and if I had lost or mutilated one I would never have been allowed in the library again. It never occurred to him that beautiful calf or morocco might contain inflammatory material.

I mention these early years and our library because no doubt my taste in reading was formed by its contents—French and English biography, history and belles lettres, with some German philosophy, out of my reach. (My grandfather had translated Kant and Stewart Houston Chamberlain.) There were no novels, no books of travel and very little poetry. I still read more biography, memoirs and letters than anything else; I like to get into some lively set, and observe its behaviour. The Encyclopaedists or Byron and his friends are supreme entertainers, but any small society will provide an interesting study in human relationships if one or two of its members can write.

They need not be professional writers—men of action not infrequently have literary gifts. We know all about Captain Scott and his companions from his own journal and Cherry Garrard's *The Worst Journey in the World*, two books I love. Here is the Englishman as he was when I was a child, of whom it has been said that his favourite words in his favourite poem were 'someone had blundered'. Scott struggled to the Pole by the most difficult route; he took insufficient rations and he went on foot because he thought it would be cruel and unfair to use dogs. The realistic foreigner who got there first raced along comfortably, his sledge drawn by dogs which he ate on the way. Would the modern Englishman hesitate between the two methods? Something seems to have happened in the past fifty years to make him more practical, less idealistic, much less respectful of animals, which are now ruthlessly sacrificed in the interests of science or expediency.

My greatest pleasure is reading to gather up material for a biography. The driest, longest book becomes a treasure chest if one is rummaging about in it for appropriate facts. The *Mémoires* of the Duc de Luynes would be unreadable to the ordinary person; they are in about sixteen volumes, pedestrian in style and written without a scrap of the sparkling malice which drives Saint-Simon's pen. But their day-to-day exactitude makes them perfectly fascinating to anybody who wants to describe Versailles in the reign of Louis XV and I raced through them at top speed when writing *Pompadour*.

Most people like reading about what they already know— there is even a public for yesterday's weather. I know about the personalities of seventeenth- and eighteenth-century Europe and I read nearly everything which appears on the subject. Much of it irritates me profoundly and I think the best books on the eighteenth century are still those written before 1914. Modern writers have dug up a few new facts, but they are too much inclined to make a long book about some hanger-on of whom Sainte-Beuve has told the essentials in a few thousand words. Their predecessors were more talented. Carlyle's *Life of Frederick the Great*, though dishonest to a comic degree about Frederick's morals, is a work of art; the secondary characters are brilliantly portrayed; Voltaire is summed up once and for all. His *French Revolution* has the grandeur of a thunderstorm. These are books I can read over and over again, and so are Macaulay's Essays, 'freighted with the spoils of the ages', and his *History of England*, Michelet's *History of France*, Sainte-Beuve's *Lundis*, and Lord Acton's Essays and Lectures. I also like the works of the Goncourts, Funck-Brentano, Pierre de Nolhac, George Saintsbury, Charles Whibley, Lenotre and others of that school, now out of fashion; nearer my own age, in the same tradition of civilized writing, I admire Lytton Strachey, Harold Nicolson, Virginia Woolf's *Common Reader* and E. M. Forster's *Abinger Harvest*.

·In the matter of novels, with few exceptions and those the greatest, I demand jokes. In my time I have enjoyed most of the French, English and Russian masterpieces, but now I hardly ever read novels. Exceptions are those of Evelyn Waugh, P. G. Wodehouse, Rose Macaulay, and E. F. Benson's Lucia books. (Will somebody not reprint these soon?) I liked *Lucky Jim* for its funniness, but it made me sad, as do all evidences of declining civilization.

I never read travel books, partly, no doubt, because I seldom travel. I cannot read criticism—I would be incapable of reading Sartre on Genet, for instance—nor can I manage literary weeklies, English or French. The English yellow Press, so much enjoyed by so many, is no good to me; when I go home I am like Rip Van Winkle, ignorant of many a household word and looming row. French popular papers have a certain charm because, long as I have lived here, I am still enchanted by such headlines as 'Excédé par le soupirant de sa gouvernante, l'octogénaire décharge son révolver sur lui.' But nothing is so bad for the eyes as newsprint.

To sum up—I like fact better than fiction and I like almost anything that makes me laugh. But my favourite book falls into neither of these categories: it is *La Princesse de Clèves*.

1961

Part Two

———

FOREIGN

Diary of a Visit to Russia, 1954

THIS account of a visit to Russia eight years ago may seem out of date; in fact, that is its only claim to interest. I was unable to publish it at the time because, incredible as it seems now, when thousands of tourists go to Russia every year, as easily as they do to France or Italy, in 1954 it was nearly impossible to get a visa. Journalists were not allowed, except those who lived there accredited to newspapers, nor were tourists. My visa was applied for by our Embassy at Paris; they handed over my passport to the Soviet Consul. A month went by and nothing happened. Then the Embassy said they had done all they could and I was advised to go myself to the Consulate, prepared for a good long wait, as people were sometimes kept there a whole day. I took a book with me. The Consulate was empty, very different from the Spanish one across the road, where about two hundred people were queuing up for visas. I gave my card to the porter and was immediately shown upstairs into a large room. A man sitting at a desk there said: 'I've been waiting for you for a month.' He opened a safe, took out my passport, duly stamped, and wished me a happy journey.

In view of the fact that I was only given a visa out of politeness to the Ambassador, he asked me not to publish anything about my visit. Much water has flowed under the bridges since then. As far as I can see, Russia must have changed more in the last eight years than in twenty before. Georgi Malenkov and Mme Malenkova are in Siberia. Sir William Hayter and Lady Hayter are in Oxford. I publish.

29th May 1954

At Helsinki I left the S.A.S. aeroplane which had taken me there from Paris. The employees of S.A.S. are even more governessy than those of B.E.A., and the passengers are continually given little lectures boringly repeated in many tongues as though anybody could not more or less grasp the gist of what they mean, and told to fasten or un-fasten or extinguish something. Not a bite of food. I was met by the Ambassador's chaplain. It was very reassuring to see his collar and nice English face waiting for me; I was starving, so he took me to a late luncheon at the airport restaurant. He then put five large parcels for the Ambassa-dress into my care and said good-bye, leaving me to get into the wrong queue, as I generally do on journeys; I was sadly trying to fill up a form when a voice said, in English, that the aeroplane for Moscow was leaving at once. So I ran across the tarmac, supposing that the other passengers would already be on board, probably rather cross with me for delaying them. A host and hostess were at the top of the stairs to greet me as I came in; apart from them the aeroplane was empty. It was very pretty, in a cottagey way, white with dark blue plush curtains and a pile carpet. The hostess wore a dark blue smock; she looked like a peasant; nothing could have been more different from the air hostess of any Western line. She busied herself making tea and caviar sandwiches while the host did the honours. 'Should you wish to rest,' he said in perfect English, 'these seats can be converted into beds—I will show you.' He struggled with one or two; nothing happened. I begged him not to bother and with some relief, I thought, he gave up. Meanwhile we had shot into the air with the minimum of fuss—no revving, no voice bossing about safety belts—no safety belts either. But we never seemed to gain any height at all and it was 'Oh do mind that tree' all the way to Moscow. So I was able to see the endless steppes very comfortably as from a train.

At Leningrad we came down. Again, no voice, the only indication that we were about to land was the sight of a field, wheeling round the windows. The airport seemed deserted. My host led me to a large room with a table, plush tablecloth, chair, cut-glass ink-stand, and silver pen; this was the Customs House, where I had to fill in a long printed form, in English, stating that I had neither this nor that, nor *wormwood roots* nor *reindeer horns* nor *spotted deers' antlers*. This struck me as so odd that I copied it into my diary, so that I would not think later that I had dreamt it. The Ambassadress's parcels were all opened. They contained salmon and cut flowers, but no horns or wormwood roots. When I said whom they were for, all became quite clear—the slight dottiness of English Ambassadresses seems to be an established fact in Russia, as in France. Of course, I would have been incapable of doing up the parcels again, but while I stood looking sadly at the string, a dear old man like a house carpenter came in and did them for me.

My host then said that I would now no doubt like to rest. I always like to, and in that way Russia suits me very well— the Russians rest more than any people I have ever met. He led me to a waiting-room, charmingly furnished with a great deal of plush, two bronze vases containing castor-oil plants, and a lovely picture of Bonny Prince Stalin with the sun setting behind him over poppies. I lay and rested on a sofa. The host walked up and down chatting happily about joy in work.

N. 'Yes, work is all right, but I don't like to be shut up indoors all day, in a factory or a bookshop.'

Host. 'Ah! Then you could be the man who puts lights for the boats on the river—but it's not very nice in winter.'

N. 'Tell me about Leningrad—I'm going to stay here a few nights on my way back.'

Host. 'I don't know it. I should only have permission to be there three days—and who can see Leningrad in three days? Where do you live?'

N. 'In Paris.'

Host. 'But you are English—why do you live in Paris?'

N. 'Because I like it.'

Host evidently thinks this is rather fishy. I found out later that people in Russia are seldom allowed to leave their own towns, let alone live in another country because they like it. (If they do, it is called choosing freedom.)

Host. 'May I look at your books?'

I hand over *Leave it to Psmith* and a paper-backed anthology called *Great Poems*.

Host borrows *Great Poems* and begins to read.

Another young man appears. 'Can we get you a room in Moscow?'

N. 'It's very kind, but I'm staying with the Ambassador.'

Young Man. 'Will he meet you, or shall I order a motor?'

N. 'Thank you so much, but he's meeting me.'

Young Man. 'Then I will telephone to the Embassy and tell them that your aeroplane is punctual. Should you wish water for your make-up I lead you to it.' He leads me to a spotless lavatory with hot water, soap and a clean linen towel. I reflect on British Railways' lavatories and indeed on the unkind, indifferent, tactless and uncomfortable treatment one so often receives when travelling in the West. It is a very nice change to be treated as a precious object for once.

Presently back to the aeroplane, which rose a few feet into the air and hedge-hopped to Moscow: My host read *Great Poems* the whole way there. When we arrived I asked him to accept the book, but he dropped it like a hot potato, saying, rather unconvincingly, that he had a copy at home. 'I wished,' he added, 'to see with what motive the editor chose these poems—it seems to have been a good motive, let's hope so.'

I was met by John Morgan. Lady Hayter came home from a dinner-party soon after I arrived at the Embassy.

'Oh, you shouldn't have done that!'

'You can't imagine how wonderful it was to have an excuse to get away.'

She hurried me off to bed. I was very tired. She explained that there was to be a Red Army parade the next day, for which they had got me an invitation. This meant getting up at 8.30 (6.30 by our time).

Sunday, 30th May

The Red Army parades usually take place twice a year, on May Day and the 7th November, to commemorate the October Revolution. But this year there was an extra one for the 300th anniversary of the union with the Ukraine. Very few foreigners and even fewer Russians have ever seen one of these parades, so I was lucky to have the chance.

I was woken up by brilliant sunshine and the sound of

singing. Looking out of my windows I saw, across the river, the unforgettable Kremlin. Nobody had ever told me how beautiful it is; a Dulac illustration to a fairy story come to life. The Embassy is almost exactly like the Travellers' Club in Paris, and it, too, was built for a cocotte, in 1893. But its ugliness is redeemed by the wonderful view. The street was full of workers, each carrying a branch or small tree covered with flowers, some real, some artificial, dancing and singing to accordions. This cheerful procession went on steadily for the next hour or two while I dressed and had my breakfast.

We left the house in the huge old Embassy Rolls-Royce, a sort of joke motor, but very comfortable, at 9.30. There was a small stand in the Red Square for members of the *Corps diplomatique* and a few Russian officials. Near us, the *chef de protocol*, one Zukoff, had a charming, pale, delicate little boy with him. He was dressed in a sailor suit and was the image of the last Cesarewitch.

Presently Malenkov and Co., in creased grey suits, looking like commercial travellers, appeared on Lenin's tomb and the show began. Massed bands punctuated by cannon fire instead of drums, endless marching troops, Migs whizzing between two church steeples; Bulganin, like a toy, standing up in a motor which dashed about from regiment to regiment, greeted by Ra-ra-ra—all as exciting as an air raid and all laid on for the commercial travellers and a few diplomats and me. No other audience allowed. The huge shop, Goum, which forms one side of the square, had not a soul in its windows. After about an hour, armed might was succeeded by the workers and their flowering trees. Several hundred thousand went by; the square looked like a vast moving garden; it was beautiful and strange and all for the benefit of Malenkov and me. It must be said, to their credit, that the rulers of Russia never make idiots of themselves like Hitler and Mussolini. No Piazza Venezia, no Nuremberg. The reality of power suffices them and they live in an atmosphere of mystery, secrecy and calm. The mystery is total. Nobody knows where they sleep. Nobody can point to a house and say 'that is Malenkov's house'. It is not even known whether or not he is married.[1] The large black motors at the disposal of the Great Men go in and out of the Kremlin (heralded by bells, all other traffic stopped) with drawn curtains. They may contain Malenkov or Malenkova, if she exists, or the body of her strangled lover, or simply the pug going out for its walk. Nobody ever knows. When a member of the Praesidium travels by air the aerodrome is shut for twenty-four hours. When Stalin died police from all over Russia were hurried into Moscow, the streets were cleared for days, and he had a quiet funeral, with a few diplomats forming the only cortege.

After the parade we lunched at the American Embassy, and then went out to Prince Yussupov's country house, now a museum. It is kept exactly as it was. 'This is the Prince's study.' Quite a big crowd of Russian tourists was being shown round. One had a feeling that they probably thought the Prince lived and died in the sixteenth century, and that they would be amazed to learn that he is very much alive today. It is a house of little architectural merit and quite devoid of beautiful furniture. The chandeliers, parquet and so on very shoddy. And yet it belonged to one of the richest men in the world. There are some Hubert Roberts, copies of Italian old masters, and some rather

[1] I heard a few months later that he is married to a very nice electrician.

charming portraits by a painter of the eighteenth century whose work I often saw in Russia, but whose name I never found out. The garden is planted with marble obelisks. One was put up whenever the Emperor came to dinner, the names of the guests inscribed in gold.

That night a dinner and dance at the French Embassy. On our way there, during a traffic block, a young man came right up to the window of the motor, gazed fixedly at me and repeatedly crossed himself. It was very strange. At dinner I sat next to M. Louis Joxe, the Ambassador, a charming person, rather donnish. He said: 'Nous sommes tous ici, comme sur le radeau de la Méduse.' The diplomats in Moscow have it on their minds that they never see anybody but each other. 'No worse', I told them, 'than living in Bath or Aix-en-Provence, before the days of motors.' (As a matter of fact, it is no worse than Paris. A few Embassies entertain French people, but it is always the same little list and on the whole the diplomats mostly see each other.) But they feel it a hardship. For a visitor like myself their conversation is fascinating, because they are all rather clever, nearly all speak Russian, and they know a great deal of what goes on. It is said to cost a million pounds a year to keep a British Embassy in Moscow, because the Government has to subsidize the rouble (giving 40 to the pound instead of 10), but the Ambassador says he thinks it is worth it. He says when we had a chargé d'affaires at Riga we knew very little of what went on inside Russia. Now it is quite different. The secretaries speak good Russian, they travel the whole time, and in the country places people are more willing to talk than in Moscow and Leningrad. Various portents are studied with interest, for instance the order in which the huge photographs of the Praesidium are placed, and which varies from time to time. Everybody at our Embassy is absorbed in Russia, old and new, its politics, history, literature and art.

Monday, 31st May

I wandered about in the morning and looked at the streets and the people. All my visit I looked and looked at the people. They seem neither happier nor sadder than in the West, and neither more nor less worried than any town dweller. (People in towns are always preoccupied. 'Have I missed the bus? Have I forgotten the potatoes? Can I get across the road?') But they appear stupid, what the French call *abruti*. What do they think? Perhaps they don't think very much, and yet they read enormously. I never saw such a country of readers—people sitting on benches, in the metro, etc., all read books (magazines seem not to exist); on the trains they have lending libraries. They are hideously ugly. Except for a few young officers, I never saw a hand-some man; there seem to be no beautiful women. They have putty faces, like Malenkov. It is nonsense to speak of Asiatics, Mongol Hordes and so on—the pretty little Tartar guards at Lenin's tomb were the only people I saw with a non-European cast of features.

Moscow is so badly planned and laid out that it seems more like a conglomeration of villages than a city. Its glories are the Kremlin and hundreds of little onion-domed churches. Many of these are falling into disrepair, some are used as cinemas (the 'Avant-Garde Cinema' is in a church), but quite a few are in full use, and are crowded on Sundays. The population of Moscow is a military secret, but is computed at seven millions. In that case it is hard to know where the people are. There are no crowded streets to

compare with Oxford Street or the Grands Boulevards, nor
does the town look big from the air. There are a few sky-
scrapers, one of which, the university, is the only skyscraper
I have ever thought beautiful though it is despised by the
experts of modern architecture. But they mostly contain
offices. The Foreign Office is in one. When the Ambassador
goes there his business takes him to the 14th floor. The lift is
on the dicky side and he constantly expects to have to run up
the stairs. In the streets little tumble-down shacks alternate
with great square blocks of flats and nineteenth-century
buildings. The courtyards here and in Leningrad are inex-
pressibly squalid, you never look through a *porte cochère* and
see something pretty—a garden, a pavilion, a fountain or a
fine façade—as in French or Italian towns. Nor do you ever
get a delicious whiff of cooking. However, there is always
some foliage. The Russians are fond of beautiful leaved
plants and are good at growing them. The double windows
even of the poorest dwellings are filled with ivy, and hundreds of varieties of rubber plants. The station at Moscow is
like the Chelsea Flower Show (without the gardening ladies,
though). As in Italy one hears music, day and night, some of
it canned, but also much singing and accordion playing,
especially on the river. When the Bishop of Fulham (Moscow
is in his diocese) went to stay at the Embassy his aeroplane
was full of peasants—at the sight of holy Moscow they all
stood up and sang.

Every house has got television, which is provided free
by the Government. This is perhaps in order to stop people
from listening to foreign wireless programmes. There are
many telephone booths in the streets; the Russians love
telephoning, which they do at great length; sometimes you
see a little group standing round the booth and passing the

receiver from hand to hand evidently all chatting to the same person. The workers are now beginning to buy motors and cameras, and a few advertisements appear in the streets, mostly for champagne and nylon stockings. Many of the women have these; the young ones wear socks. Their shoes are very decent and their clothes about the level of Glasgow or a poor suburb of Paris; quite adequate and perfectly hideous. The women wear men's tweed jackets over cotton dresses. The young ones are made up, paint their nails (about twice a year by the look of them) and do their hair like the London workers during the air raids, up in front and down behind; not much brushing. In the aggregate, they smell like a poor London or Paris crowd. All this applies to everybody; you never see an exception. So the Russians can tell a foreign woman at sight. They often came up to me and asked questions—at first I thought they were asking the way, but the Ambassador said that, although the Kremlin clock is generally visible, they were probably asking the time, in order to see my watch. Watches and clocks have always fascinated them. In a gallery a woman came up to me, whispered in my ear 'Beautiful' and hurried away. They love talking to one, which they do in French mostly, but it frightens them; I saw this over and over again. Many people known to have associated with foreigners disappeared during the Purge.

There are many drunks in the streets. They reel about, clinging to sober or less drunk companions, hugging the lamp posts or simply rolling in the gutter like figures in a farce. Nobody pays any attention to them. Sailors nearly always seem to be drunk.

The Russians cannot count, and I have the impression that they are totally uninterested in money. (I know the symptoms because I cannot count myself, and am also not really interested in money. In my mind the things which money brings, as well as the work which brings money, seem unconnected with it.) In the shops, where, of course, the salesmen do not care whether they sell or not, since it makes no difference to them, all the shops being State-owned, each girl has rows of beads, like a baby, on which to do the addition. Incidentally there is nothing one could possibly want to buy—the goods are about the standard of our chain stores. At the hotel in Leningrad I had the same breakfast every morning and each time the bill was different; even I could see that at luncheon and dinner the waiter always added it up wrong. In all the time I was in Russia nobody accepted a tip. At the theatre, where it is obligatory to leave your coat in the cloakroom (I was told this is because of the awful smell of badly cured furs in winter), neither the cloakroom attendant nor the *ouvreuse* expect or would take a tip, nor would taxi-drivers, the servants in the hotel, or at the Embassy. Now, if the love of money is the root of all evil, it is perhaps the root of a certain amount of humanity, too, and this total detachment has something frightening about it. It was the single thing about the Russians that struck me most. Have they always been like this—has communism produced it or is it because there is so little to buy? I would like to know.

The children are splendid. They look much more wide awake and better dressed than the grown-ups, are evidently well fed and loved. The Ambassador thinks they are the great hope for the future. Driving in the country one often passes a lorry full going for picnics, looked after by a nurse or a schoolteacher. In Leningrad I saw children in well-kept prams apparently pushed by nannies.[1] In Moscow my bathroom looked out on to a kinder-garten—the children all seemed well and happy, they played card games in a yard during the break. In the streets they make chalk squares on the pavement as they do in London.

On Monday afternoon we went to a gallery of Russian art, mostly containing nineteenth-century pictures, many of which 'tell a story'. They are skilfully painted in great detail and provide a document of pre-Revolution daily life, showing the clothes which the bourgeois, his children and his servants wore, and the poky little wooden rooms with low ceilings, no curtains or carpets, in which they lived. The furniture is portrayed in detail down to the very wastepaper-basket; all is simple and austere, rather naïve. An aristocrat will be dressed in silk or velvet, a pack of cards not far off and the bailiffs waiting outside the door. The more popular of these pictures are very droll. There is one of Ivan the Terrible killing his son. But Ivan is being rehabilitated, so the picture is now called Ivan the Good rendering first aid to his son. A picture of bears gambolling in a wood is reproduced all over Russia, and so are the Three Bogateers (sort of Vikings) in helmets and shields. There are many conversation pieces depicting Lenin and Stalin, always in a sunset glow. Lenin and Stalin, who in life hated each other and seldom met, and who in death lie together like a dreadful old married couple, have passed into Soviet mythology as having enjoyed one of the greatest, purest and most fruitful friendships of all time. There is a picture of the last days of Hitler: three German generals are carousing on champagne when Hitler, wild-eyed, bursts in upon them. They are too drunk to care.

[1] But the Ambassador said, 'Not nannies, grannies.'

It is the fashion in the West to mock at the nineteenth-century Russian school. A second look, however, might bring a more favourable verdict. There are many ridiculous pictures; there are also some poetic landscapes and excellent portraits. The last two rooms in this museum contain eikons.

Monday evening. A party at the Embassy. Faces beginning to become familiar to me. This dance was notable because Lady Hayter had managed to induce members of the ballet to come and perform, the first time any Russian artist had been to a foreign house since the Purge. They were not very good—in fact, by any standards at all they were very bad—but nobody minded that; it was such a rarity to see them there. They refused, however, to come and drink champagne after the performance. There were no Russian guests—that would have been amazing indeed.

Officials sometimes come to the Embassy (for the Queen's birthday party for instance). When they do they are always startled by the portrait in the dining-room, of King George V, which they take for the Tsar. The only time Stalin ever went there he is supposed to have walked straight out in a rage on seeing the picture. It is rather odd that they all know so exactly what the Tsar looked like, as no pictures of him seem to exist any more in Russia.

Tuesday, 1st June

Nothing special—in the evening we went to the station—unchanged since the days of Tolstoy—to see off one of the secretaries and his wife, who were leaving. The whole *corps diplomatique* seemed to be here, and the French Ambassador was heard to say that they had had 'une bonne gare'.

Diary of a Visit to Russia, 1954

Wednesday, 2nd June

M. and Mme Le Roy, old friends from Free French days,
took me to the Pushkin museum. It is the class of a French or
English provincial museum. It apparently owns some good
Impressionists, but these are not shown. Mme Le Roy had
just had her fifth baby in a Moscow hospital and gave a most
gruesome account of the experience. No anaesthetic.
'Please don't cry,' they said; 'you'll upset the others.'

Cocktail party at the Italian Embassy, and then to the
Bolshoi theatre to see a ballet called *The Fountain*. The
music, I believe, has been described by Mr Sackville West
as Tchaikowsky and Benzedrine—just suits me. The story
is of a beautiful Countess Potocka ravished away from
Lançut by a Tartar King. These names were on the
programme.

Curiously enough, we are meant to be on the side of the
charming, decadent Poles, in white skating-boots, who are
attacked in the middle of a garden-party by the wicked
little yellow men. (The Ambassador says Russians even
now unwillingly revere the Poles, more civilized Slavs than
themselves. He also says that actors representing Poles
on the Russian stage always wear white skating-boots.) The
dancing seemed to me splendid, especially in the Tartar
dances—the ballerina, a charming and romantic-looking
girl called Kondryativa, is supposed to be the coming star
and is preferred by some people to Ulanova (whom I never
saw). An Englishman who was there said that Margot Fon-
teyn wouldn't get into the corps de ballet in Russia, great
nonsense no doubt. A good deal of the enjoyment, however,
is spoilt by the horrible vulgarity of the décor—Dorothy
Perkins wherever you look. The sets are changed as often as
possible, so that the entr'actes are many and long. The

Russians despised the *Comédie française* for only having one set to each play. The Bolshoi is not, as I had half expected, a sort of Festival Hall, but a huge, splendid, nineteenth-century opera house.

Thursday, 3rd June

Miss Shepherd, of the Embassy, took me to the Lenin library. As I have been told that any fine French book which has disappeared is always assumed to be in Russia, I hoped to see some interesting specimens. This was explained to the man who took us in charge and he asked another man to get out some fine French bindings. Meanwhile I had a look at the card index, which is in Roman lettering. Of course, I looked up Mitford—they have got several editions of Mary Russell M., and my great-grandfather's (reactionary) *History of Greece*. So I assume that they must have all the English classics, however obscure. I turned to Molière—there are about twenty early editions. Presently we were taken to a small room where a table was covered with boxes—this looked hopeful until they were opened. I was then reverently shown about six nineteenth-century French morocco bindings, deadly dull, a small keepsake album bound in wood and green plush, and an interesting Russian binding of the seventeenth century. I hardly knew what to say, my natural desire to please fighting with a determination not to let them get away with it. I said: 'But we know that the Great Catherine owned some beautiful morocco.' They replied: 'We in Russia do not care for the outside of books; it is their message that interests us.' It was now luncheon-time, so I gave up. The Lenin library is a huge glass building which, from some angles, very much spoils the lovely Kremlin skyline. Inside, the green plants run riot and in places it looks like the hot-house at Kew. I understand that a thousand people read there every day—all the reading-rooms I saw were quite full.

The Tomb. At five o'clock, when I was having a little rest, John Morgan came and said we had permission now to go to the Tomb. It so happened that I had never seen a dead person, so the dreadful old married couple gave me quite a jump. The setting is strongly reminiscent of Mme. Tussaud's but the exhibits are not at all like wax-works. They seem most lively, and Lenin looks at one out of the corner of his eye, which is just a little open. As I passed Stalin I could not help remembering that, wicked as he may have been, the dear old soul did save our bacon. But for him where would we be now? There were many Chinese with us in the queue. The Russians stand in it for six hours, but foreigners who have a card go in after about five minutes. All is privilege in that country.

Prince Igor at the Bolshoi.

Friday, 4th June

At 10.15 James Bennett (3rd Sec.) came to take me to the Kremlin. It is very difficult to get in and there were doubts until the last moment as to whether I should be allowed. The heatwave of the first days had quite disappeared and it was cold like January. We stood in a biting wind outside the gate, waiting—so we were informed—for some Ethiopians. I said to Mr Bennett: 'Do tell them its quite useless to wait for Ethiopians'—and, in fact, they never turned up. However, the Persian Minister, a most charming, jolly man, did, and we advanced into the dreaded precincts. I won't describe what we saw as it can be found in any guide-book. The visit lasts three hours; one could happily spend days there, since

there are treasures beyond imagination. Much too long a
time is spent reverently looking at the largest cannon in
the world which has never been fired, the largest bell in the
world which has never been rung, and the hall of the
Supreme Soviet which is exactly like any other lecture hall.
I was saddened to learn that half the delegates are women.
Russian women seem to be far more earnest, intransigent
and impervious to charm than the chaps. They are like
Conservative women M.P.s, French highbrow duchesses
and American fashion editresses rolled into super-govs.
I would not care to be in their power. At the Kremlin
we had two women guides—one was a super-gov., but
the other was a dear. In the Cathedral, super-gov. said:
'You see now we have electric light here; in the bad old
days it was candles.' I said: 'Candles are prettier.' The
dear said, whispering in my ear when super-gov. had gone
on, 'Much prettier.'

Presently super-gov. said: 'Now we will rest', and we
dumped sadly down within sight of the museum; at least
another quarter of an hour wasted.

In the museum there are many cases containing silver sent
by various kings to the emperors—including a pair of wine
bottles from Queen Elizabeth to Ivan the Terrible and a
whole service made in Paris (Germain?) for Count Orloff.
Lady Kelly, in her book on Russia, invites us to turn with
relief from all this 'heavy hand-made French silver' to the
charming little objects by Fabergé: little horrors, I thought.
The silver is labelled by weight. I asked super-gov. about a
pair of Louis XIV consoles; she replied: 'Russian workman-
ship of the nineteenth century, weighing X number of
kilos.'

In the afternoon we went to Tolstoy's town house. It is

like the houses in Russian pictures, very simple, built of wood, a china stove forming part of the wall of each room. Here he spent twenty winters, having built himself what my father used to call a 'child-proof' room—though Tolstoy's was probably more wife than child proof. The dining-room table is laid for dinner and the drawing-room table for tea—china and furniture unchanged since he lived there. The beds are all made up, nice linen sheets trimmed with coarse lace. One is shown over by an old woman who was part of the Tolstoy household—she tells all sorts of fascinating domestic details.

Then Lady Hayter and I went to a dress show in one of the big shops. We paid five shillings to go in. Another super-gov. gave a little pep talk on how it is the duty of Soviet wives and daughters to look as attractive as possible, and then the hideous mannequins galumphed with squeaky shoes on to the stage. The clothes were incredibly dreary: skimpy, badly cut, hems all lengths. The simple expedient of going round them with a tape measure had not been resorted to. We became rather giggly, but controlled ourselves until one of the mannequins began to undo her bodice. At Paris shows this is quite usual. 'L'heure avance' and the day dress becomes suitable for cocktails or dinner. Rather a grubby idea, I always think, but practical. But in this case out bounced a large naked breast; super-gov. then explained that the dress was designed for a nursing mother. Seized with helpless giggles, we took ourselves off.

Then we went to a picture dealer and saw many huge canvases of contemporary art: white rabbits among blue-bells, kittens peeping out of a jack-boot, conversation pieces of the old married couple and portraits of the Bonny Prince.

These pictures fetch hundreds of pounds and sell like hot cakes.

Home in time for a cocktail party at the Embassy in honour of two English musicians, Messrs Loveday and Cassini.

I had asked to meet some Soviet writers, but a message came from the Ministry of Culture that the Soviet writers had gone to the country, on the 28th May, to write. It seems they are picked up in buses, in alphabetical order (as it were Mauriac, Maurois, Mitford, Mithois) and carted off to a dacha, where they are obliged to show up 2,000 words a day during the whole summer. A woman from the State publishing house came to this party and I got her into a corner. She was yet another super-gov. and I received a very cold look from her small blue eye. Russians, like Americans, tend to loathe me on sight. 'How many copies would you sell here of a popular novel?' I asked. She replied fifty million.

N. 'How absolutely wonderful. I can't wait to come and be a Soviet writer.'

Super-gov. (clearly not taking to the idea). 'This has its good side and its bad.'

N. 'Well it can't have a bad side for the writer. Do tell me the name of a book which has sold like this.'

Super-gov. '*Cement*.' She added that if I liked she would take me, on Monday, to the home of a worker, so that I could see for myself how it would be full of books. I had visions of a wretched man's house being requisitioned and bookshelves being run up the whole week-end. I said I was leaving on Monday. She asked if I had seen any workers' dwellings and I said no there are plenty of them at home, I've come here to see the museums.

When I told the Danish Ambassador, as a joke, about the fifty million copies of *Cement*, he said that a certain Danish writer, fellow traveller, sells six million copies in the Soviet Union.

Every day we received *Pravda* in English. While I was in Moscow a novel appeared called *The Seasons* which got a long review. The book sounds rather fascinating; it is about a family of revolutionaries who had a thrilling life during the early years of the revolution and have now settled down to a dreary, humdrum old age. The *Pravda* critic disapproved. '*The Seasons* is well observed and well written. This is quite so. But this novel does not summon to anything, nor struggle with anything.' Exactly what reviewers say about my books.

There was also an article on religion. The theme of it was 'Of course, in the old days before science, when people died, they liked to think of a future life. Babies were baptized as a sort of purification, because in those days children often died. But now we no longer need these superstitions. . . .'

That night, *Cinderella* at the Bolshoi.

Saturday, 5th June

In the morning I went with Mr Morgan on the metro, which is certainly very splendid, strange to Western eyes because there are no advertisements. The people were all buried in their books. I wish I knew what they were reading.

In the evening the English musicians gave a concert of Elgar and Ireland. There was enormous applause and as many encores as the artists would give. The Ambassador says the Russians will sit through anything sooner than go back to their dismal homes. Then we dined in a restaurant—

not, alas, Cocktail Hall. Cocktail Hall is where all the young decadents meet, drink cocktails, chew gum, listen to jazz and pretend to be Americans. They speak of the Kremlin as the White House, of Goum as Saks Fifth Avenue and so on, with an American accent. It is all considered very fast and daring. But the Ambassador refused to take me there, on the grounds that it will soon be raided by the police.

Sunday, 6th June

To Zagorsk, the great monastery about sixty miles from Moscow, so wonderfully described by Théophile Gautier in his *Voyage en Russie* and quite unchanged since he saw it. Its walled enclosure contains three or four churches, a huge refectory, a bell tower, the Patriarch's palace and a seminary, for which the Patriarch says he gets as many young priests as he wants. Zagorsk is one of the most stunningly beautiful places I ever saw. There are treasures of gold and silver and jewels in the churches and the museum—among many other things is a huge silver dish, decorated with dolphins, sent by Charles I to the Patriarch of his day. The canopy over the body of St Serge is of seventeenth-century silver. A crowd waited for holy water, which gushes up from a gold receptacle. Mercifully the Germans never got to Zagorsk as it is east of Moscow.

Monday, 7th June: Whit Monday

Another expedition, to Gorki, the house where Lenin spent much of his time after he was shot at and wounded in 1918 and where, in 1924, he died. It is too pretty; built about 1800, of wood, with elegant balconies, painted yellow and white. We were shown round by a young man who was so penetrated with a sort of religious emotion that sometimes he could hardly speak. 'On this very bench Vladimir Ilyich used to sit, with the Comrade Stalin.' The imaginary friendship of these two is very much built up at Gorki. There are photographs of them chatting together, said by the Ambassador to be faked, and the young man showed us a telephone installed, he said, specially for Vladimir Ilyich to speak with the Comrade Stalin in Moscow. On the walls there are photographs of Lenin's funeral. Six out of the eight pall-bearers have since been liquidated; they have also been erased from the photographs, so that it looks as if Stalin and one other man are carrying the coffin between them—making a very odd effect. As we drove through the countryside, on these various excursions, I was able to see the state of the villages. They are sadder and more backward than those of Spain or Ireland. Women go to the well with two buckets on a yoke; roads are only tracks, deep in mud; goats everywhere, sure sign of poverty and feckless-ness; no gardens.

A dinner-party, followed by another English concert—Ireland and Elgar again—more wild applause.

Tuesday, 8th June

I flew, in the pretty little hedge-hopping aeroplane, to Leningrad. This time there were three or four passengers, all being sick. The hostess too busy with them to chat to me; there was no host this time. I gobbled up an amusing book called *Bears in the Caviar* which the Hayters had lent me. In the end I read it four times, because the Leningrad bookshops had nothing in English or French except Jack London, at an enormous price.

I was met at the airport by the young man who had asked where I would stay in Moscow; he had a motor waiting

which took us to the Hotel Astoria. Here he handed me over
to the Intourist people, who all spoke English. They asked
if I wanted to go to the Opera and what excursions, if any,
they could arrange for me. I said yes to the Opera and said I
would spend the following day at the Hermitage and then
see what I felt like doing the day after. I went straight off
to the Hermitage and began to orientate myself for an hour,
when it shut.

When I got back I found the hall of the Astoria piled high
with American luggage; great cabin trunks labelled to
addresses in the States. The Intourist people were being
run off their feet by the owners of this luggage, nasty-looking
Americans, very rude. This seemed as odd as the wormwood
roots. I learnt afterwards that American Communists
manage to get to Russia from European ports without
having their passports stamped, so that the people at home
are none the wiser.

The hotel itself is full of charm. My bedroom was
furnished like a Victorian drawing-room, it had a very
comfortable sofa and writing-table with bronze ink-stand
filled with ink; plenty of writing paper. The water in
my bathroom was hot all the time, though not always
quite clean. The rooms gave on to a big landing, with
furniture and pictures, and here sat, day and night, three
or four housemaids in muslin caps which look like wreaths.
They had got a wireless set, but usually preferred to chat.
They were kind and thoughtful. The first night I was
rather cold and put my coat on my bed—next day I found
two extra blankets lying folded on the sofa. Very comfortable bed.

Went to *Sleeping Beauty*. It was long, the performance less
good than in Moscow, but the audience interested me. The

people seemed more wide awake than the Muscovites. There were many young officers, who looked clever, amused and very nice indeed. Both the Leningrad theatres are extremely elegant. I found the English musicians during an entr'acte, wandering about in a state of euphoria. Mr Cassini looked as if he had just come from a casino, his pockets literally bulged with huge banknotes. They had received 10,000 roubles each for a fifteen minutes broadcast. 'Enough to buy two small cars,' said Mr Loveday. I pointed out that nobody wants two small cars, though you might want a large and a small one. He wasn't listening: 'To think I do my own washing up in the Fulham road.' I said we ought all to come and live here, that's what it is.

Wednesday, 9th June

Dinner the night before having been literally uneatable (worse than railway food in England), I woke up very hungry and had eggs for breakfast. Like everything in the bedrooms the breakfast was well presented. The restaurant, however, is pathetic—dirty, awful waiting and impossible food. I saw one of the waiters drinking out of a decanter. The meat plate is always left while one eats one's pudding. I went to the Hermitage as soon as it opened and was there all day. Everybody knows that it is the largest museum in the world, and what extraordinary treasures it contains. I concentrated on the French things, a collection about as big as the Wallace, with less furniture (and much of what there is horribly regilded), but more pictures, bibelots, statuettes and silver. I was particularly anxious to see the silver and was disappointed to find that the enormous room which contains it was roped off for cleaning. I decided to wait until the next day, when I hoped it would be opened again.

Foreign

A woman who spoke English kindly took me to the Impressionists, which are not quite easy to find. She said: 'We will make a detour to see your great Duke Wellington, who took part in our first patriotic war.' There he was, to be sure, painted by some sub-Lawrence and surrounded by Russian generals.

The Impressionists are very fine indeed, especially a Monet of a woman in white on a hot, hot country day, a small Renoir portrait of a girl—some early Picassos. But rather few are shown. There are some nineteenth-century French pictures of the school of Delaroche, notably one of Oliver Cromwell opening the coffin of Charles I and gazing at his severed head. This had a large and admiring crowd round it.

I wandered a little in the town, which is beautiful and unspoilt—exactly like illustrations to Orme's *St Petersburg*. A heatwave had suddenly begun, the temperature shot up to the eighties and people crowded out to hold their pale faces to the sun. The musicians, whom I met in the hotel, had been to Peterhof. They said the park is splendid, but the Germans had put time bombs in all the rooms before leaving so that the decoration is for ever destroyed. I knew from the Hayters that the same had happened at the Summer Palace and decided not to bother about an excursion. I was fascinated by the Hermitage anyhow, although getting very tired. I hate vodka and can't drink Soviet wine; this made my meals impossible; my digestion began to give out.

Madame Butterfly at the Opera. I sat next to a dear fellow who gave me to understand that he was from Tashkent, and we sobbed together, though unable to converse. From time to time I tried to rub it in that Pinkerton is American, not English. (I often think what a mercy this is.) I never heard anything like the boo-hooing all over the theatre. Mr Raymond Mortimer once said in an article that audiences laugh aloud at plays, but do not cry aloud—he has clearly never been to *Madame Butterfly* in Leningrad. When I came out, into broad daylight, people were still sitting about on benches, reading their books, holding their faces to the rays of the midnight sun. This hunger for light is very pathetic.

Thursday, 10th June

I went to the Hermitage as soon as it opened (11 a.m.) and found my way back to the French silver. This time the door to the room was shut. So I sat down among Claude Lorrains and demanded a director. After a great deal of consultation between the old women who sit guarding the rooms, one of them went off and fetched a charming person who spoke French. She unlocked the door and showed me the cases full of silver and silver gilt, huge seventeenth-century wine coolers, etc. etc. She was very friendly. I told her how the silver in the Kremlin is labelled only according to weight and she laughed. She had never been inside the Kremlin. When we parted she said, 'Je trouve que vous êtes courageuse de venir toute seule à Léningrad, sans parler un mot de Russe.' I replied that it is 'pénible de ne pas pouvoir s'expliquer'. 'Oui, et seule—seule.'

In the afternoon and evening I walked round the town, went to the shops and so on—saw the Falconnet Peter the Great. It was my last day—on Friday the 11th, I flew home, carrying two large buckets of caviar. As soon as I arrived I summoned a few friends to a caviar feast. I have never given such a successful party. Nobody threw me a word or asked about my voyage; they guzzled in concentrated silence.

Vive Le Président

'Il ne faut jamais se donner des coups de pied à soi-même' is a French proverb, but no people in the world give themselves so many kicks as the French. The disobliging and often unfair things that are said about France by her neighbours have always been said first, and more bitterly, here in Paris. The French denigrators of France had a field day during the Presidential election. The papers wanted a speedy result, which could have been reached only by the election either of President Auriol or of M. Herriot. But M. Auriol did not want to stand again, for private reasons, and M. Herriot is far too ill. So the Deputies and Senators took their time to choose a President in whom they have confidence; they were unaffected by the rising hysteria of the Press.

Just as it is impossible, in a Spanish town, to keep away from the bullfight, so, as excitement mounted and nobody talked of anything else, I found myself on the road to Versailles. It was lined the whole way from Paris by a *haie d'honneur* composed of policemen and Republican guards. Poor hedge, it wilted rather as the days went on. The Congress was held in a semicircular hall of the same hideous date as the Chambre des Députés, which it very much resembles.

But the atmosphere was not at all the same. In the Chambre the parties vote in blocks, so that individual mem-

bers need not attend. The result is that unless some fine
oratory is expected the house is almost empty. At Versailles
each member must go up to the platform and put his secret
vote into an urn. More than 900 Deputies and Senators were
therefore obliged to be present all the time. Conscious that
the eye of television was upon them, the old ones mounted
the tribune with jaunty step, casting away sticks and deaf-
aids as if they were at Lourdes. The young put on a thoughtful, statesmanlike air. In the Chambre the Gaullists are the
bad boys, always joking and laughing and in trouble with
their seniors; at Versailles the difficulty and delay, the
rowdiness and *manifestations houleuses,* all came from the
middle parties. The Gaullists sat throughout the congress
looking like cats who have swallowed a canary.

I was put in a gallery with the Ministers' wives, various
chefs de cabinets and friends of the *bureau.* '*De nombreuses
élégances féminines*', said the papers. These elegant creatures soon established a system of signals with the loved
ones below, rather like that between bookies at a race
meeting. It worked very well, and they knew the result of
each *scrutin* before anybody, almost before the votes could
have been counted—'He needs another thirty.' 'He has
lost sixty.'

Days went by. Television dropped the Congress in
favour of bridge lessons and Christmas carols. The
Deputies began to behave as if they were back in the
Palais Bourbon, sleeping, or reading *Paris Match.*

The *élégantes* in the gallery compared notes about their
increasingly desperate position with regard to Christmas—
presents unbought, tree ungarnished, hundreds of cards
unopened. The wife of one of the candidates proudly stated
that she had never given a Christmas present in her life.

Nobody was sorry when soon afterwards her husband withdrew from the fray. Christmas, in France, has become almost as sacred as in England. The ladies were at the end of their repertory of hats; Madame Cornu and Madame Jacquinot reappeared in their white satin and Parma velvet of the opening session. The Bishop of Versailles waived the Friday fast, so that the Deputies could be sustained by a light luncheon: *feuilleté de bécassine aux truffes, turbot sauce hollandaise, chevreuil grand veneur, poulet rôti, salade, fromage, petits fours.* In spite of this: 'J'en ai assez de la vie de château,' said M. Louis Vallon, the wag of the Palais Bourbon.

At last, the day before Christmas Eve, a new atmosphere was noticeable. M. Laniel had retired, M. Jacquinot had failed, a Vice-President of the Senate, M. Coty, had become the Right-wing candidate. The *scrutin* was put off from 4 p.m. to 6 p.m.; I went to have a little chat with my friend Mlle Joly in the library. This is one of the most beautiful rooms I know, built by a young Army officer in 1750 to be the Duc de Choiseul's Foreign Office. It contains thousands of volumes bound in morocco with royal coats of arms and many colour plate books. Mlle Joly said it seemed strange that none of the Senators or Deputies, during the days they had now spent just the other side of the road had thought of looking in here. The fact is few people know about this library. When I got back to the assembly I found M. Raymond Rödel sitting next to me. This was very significant; the Président des Fêtes de France is not the man to waste an afternoon. The race-course signals were working at top speed, and rumours poured in from the *coulisses.* It was to be a straight fight between Messieurs

Coty and Naegelen. Would the M.R.P. vote for M. Coty? If this session decided nothing the Gaullists would refuse to vote again until the parties came to an agreement. The signallers prophesied that M. Coty would lack about ten votes, and there would immediately be another *scrutin*. They were right, as usual.

After the second *scrutin* there was no need for signals. *Ça y était.* The President of the Chambre announced the result; the Assembly burst into wild cheering, gave another cheer for M. Naegelen, and sang the 'Marseillaise'. The election was over. The Deputies had taken their time and had elected the man whom the present situation requires: an Independent, a life-long Parliamentarian, not too rich, with a sound provincial background and decent family life. In short, a man typical of the best French Presidents under the Third Republic. As the wives of the defeated candidates went downstairs they told each other how very, very sorry they felt for 'cette pauvre chère Madame Coty'.

1953

Some Rooms for Improvement

'WHAT became of that man I used to see sitting at the end of your table?' somebody asked the famous eighteenth-century Paris hostess, Mme Geoffrin.

'He was my husband. He is dead.' It is the epitaph of all such husbands. The hostess of a salon (the useful word *salonnière*, unfortunately, is an Anglo-Saxon invention) must not be encumbered by family life, and her husband, if he exists, must know his place.

The salon was invented by the Marquise de Rambouillet at the beginning of the seventeenth century. She was half Italian, born in 1588 in Rome, where her father was the French Ambassador. (It is worth noting that the French word derives from the Italian *salone*.) At the age of twelve she married the Marquis de Rambouillet, who provided her with a name, a house, and an income and, but for her, would never have been heard of.

Mme de Rambouillet began at the beginning: she designed and built a house in Paris suitable for the form of gathering she was to inaugurate. The Hôtel de Rambouillet stood on the present site of the Magasin du Louvre in the Rue de Rivoli. It was a complete departure from the existing type of nobleman's residence, where the reception-rooms, painted dark brown or red, were so pompous, huge and dreary that it had become the fashion for women to receive in their bedrooms, since these were the only intimate places in the house. Mme de Rambouillet designed a series of small sitting-rooms leading out of each other and giving on to a beautiful garden filled, in summer, with orange and oleander trees; the rooms were cosy; they inspired confidences and long leisurely hours of talk. The blue room, hung with blue and white brocade on a gold ground, was her masterpiece and is famous in the history of house decoration.

When Mme de Rambouillet's house was ready, she filled it with people chosen because they could talk amusingly—another innovation. Instead of inviting only noblemen, she steered clear of court circles and surrounded herself with writers and artists of middle-class origin. Her literary star, Voiture, was the son of a wine merchant.

Mme de Rambouillet was not herself well educated (this applies to many of the women who have had salons), but she was attractive, had a talent for conversation, and made her house so gay and amusing that everybody longed to be invited there. Though she insisted on politeness, she was a seventeenth- and not an eighteenth-century person, and like all her contemporaries she loved a practical joke. Voiture wrote her a sonnet; she had it printed and sewn into an old anthology of verse which she then lent to the poet. When he came upon his poem he supposed it must be something he had once read, subconsciously remembered, and rewritten as his own. He was positively haunted by the affair until at last Mme de Rambouillet confessed all. To pay her back he got hold of two dancing bears which he brought into the blue room while she was reading poetry aloud. She suddenly perceived the addition to her audience reflected in a looking-glass—we can imagine the result, screams of terror followed by screams of rage and then by screams of laughter.

Society in those days had its childish side. But if the tone of the Hôtel de Rambouillet was high-spirited, it was also serious. Not only was the company fond of intellectual parlour games—Voiture had a talent for setting rhymed conundrums—but the French language was under constant discussion. (The French Academy, whose function it is to preserve the language, was founded in 1655.) Some contemporaries, jealous perhaps, were critical of the Rambouillet set. But the French aristocracy of that day had few interests beyond hunting and warfare and cared little for things of the mind; the fact is that French conversation was first brought to a fine art at the Hôtel de Rambouillet. European civilization owes a debt to this Marquise.

Mme de Rambouillet's successors have been legion. The most famous of her immediate ones was Mlle de Scudéry (1607-1701), herself a member of the Rambouillet set. She was a very clever person, well educated in every sense of the word. She spoke Spanish and Italian, painted, danced, wrote best-selling novels, and at the same time knew all about farming and gardening; she could cook and sew, make scents and preserves, and was an excellent sick-nurse. She was ugly even in her youth, and virtuous until her dying day (at ninety-four). She liked men better than women, however, and used to say that when women are together there is no interesting conversation: it always comes back to ribbons, gossip, or servants. The moment a man appears the tone changes. When men are together the talk may lack gaiety and lightness, but it is never dull—in short, we need them more than they need us. For conversation to

be perfect, she felt, it should touch on many different subjects, never resting heavily on one; there must be no bitter-
ness or disagreeable teasing, and it must never be improper.
'Esprit de politesse, esprit de joie.' Mlle de Scudéry enter-
tained every Saturday; her guests included Mlle de Montpensier, la Grande Mademoiselle, as well as Mme de
Sévigné and Huet, one of the most learned men of the age.

Then there was the Marquise de Sablé (1599-1678),
another hostess who moved in the same circles as Mlle de
Scudéry. The bright particular star of her salon was the
Duc de La Rochefoucauld, her lover. In 1662 Mme de Sablé
abandoned the world, made a general confession, and
entered a convent. Her guests and her Duke were taken over
by the Comtesse de La Fayette (1634-93). Nobody ever
knew whether Mme de La Fayette and La Rochefoucauld
were lovers, but he visited her every day until his death, and
as their mutual friend Bussy-Rabutin remarked, in such
cases there is always love. Mme de La Fayette's husband
lived in the country, so he did not interfere with this relationship whatever it may have been, but her little dog was
furiously jealous of the Duke. To this day ghostly barks are
heard in the old house in the Rue de Vaugirard at the very
hour when he used regularly to pay his call.

Other members of Mme de La Fayette's salon included her lifelong friend, the famous and delightful
Marquise de Sévigné, Huet, Segrais the poet, Mignard the
painter, the Marquise de Thianges (sister of Mme de
Montespan, Louis XIV's mistress), and a flighty young
couple, the Marquis and Marquise de Coulanges. Mme de
Coulange's confessor used to say: 'This lady's sins are a
series of epigrams.' The great middle-class writers of the
day, such as Racine, Molière, Pascal, and Boileau, do not

seem ever to have been invited to the Rue de Vaugirard; La Fontaine went there once, but his manners were supposed to have been uncouth and he was not a success. Two great works of art, however, were the direct result of Mme de La Fayette's gatherings: her own novel, *La Princesse de Clèves*, and La Rochefoucauld's *Maximes*. Both these wonderful books were submitted at all stages to members of the salon to be polished and repolished, the historical details for *La Princesse de Clèves*, which is set in the court of Henri II, were lovingly studied; everybody was immersed in all the histories and memoirs that could be found.

Unlike Mme de Rambouillet, Mme de La Fayette was fond of high society and would really have liked a place at the Court, which was now at Versailles; unfortunately, her two greatest friends, La Rochefoucauld and Cardinal de Retz, were looked on with no good eye by Louis XIV, since they had both taken part in the rebellion of the Fronde. Mme de Thianges knew that Mme de La Fayette longed to be received by the King; so she had a model made of her friend's salon with wax figures of the usual guests and presented this charming toy, which she called La Chambre du Sublime, to her nephew the Duc du Maine, in front of Louis XIV and the whole Court. The King was intrigued and amused; he invited Mme de La Fayette to Versailles and himself showed her all the sights. If death had come upon her at that moment, she would have died happy.

The eighteenth century differed from the seventeenth in manners, customs, and thought. People became more refined in their habits (cleaner for one thing), the minor arts were cultivated as never before or since, and the art of conversation rose to its zenith. A salon which could be said to bridge

these two epochs was that of Mme de Lambert (1647-1733).
For twenty years she was happily married to a rich banker;
when he died she set up house in a wing of the Palais
Mazarin (now the Bibliothèque Nationale), where she received society people and writers. It was said that she gave
the *ton* to a new era. Like many good hostesses, she had an
austere side to her character: hers was the only house in
Paris where no gambling was allowed; she frowned, too, on
improper talk, which, she said, was the sign of a deranged
heart and was not the least bit clever. Religion, even if one
did not quite believe in it, was a decent sentiment much to
be encouraged. She advised her son to have mistresses
superior to himself, so that he would be kept up to the mark.
'With one's equals one is apt to relax (l'esprit s'assoupit).'
'Be kind to your servants,' she said; 'they are your unlucky
friends.' She laid down two excellent rules for conversation:
no anecdotes; never tell the same thing twice—not only not
to the same people, but never at all. Talk should pour out
quite fresh; once something has been said, the dew is
off it.

The most famous of eighteenth-century salons—perhaps,
indeed, of all French salons—was that of the Marquise du
Deffand. Her long life (1697-1780) lasted from a year after
the death of Mme de Sévigné to nine years before the French
Revolution, and during all that time she hardly left Paris.
She was beautiful, highly intelligent, and very funny. As a
child she received almost no education; afterwards, as
autodidacts usually do, she cursed her parents for this,
saying that she would not care to be young again unless she
could be sure of having a worldly, clever man as tutor.
She was engaged in a perpetual fight against boredom—the
only enemy she ever feared. The trouble was that she

could not believe that anything really mattered. A practising
Roman Catholic, she wished with all her heart to have faith;
it seemed impolite to doubt, and, like Mme de Lambert, she
regarded religion as a decent sentiment. But faith eluded
her. For most of her life she had the same attitude towards
love. Her husband bored her and she soon managed to get
rid of him; thereafter she practised love without believing
in it, because it was the usual thing to do in her world. She
had love affairs with the Regent and others who moved in
the same set; then she settled down, apparently for life,
with Charles Hénault, President of the Paris *parlement*
and great friend of Voltaire's. Their affair lasted forty years,
but was always rather tepid. When the President was old
and failing and so absent-minded that half the time he did
not know where he was, she made him talk about another
woman he had loved, Mme de Castelmoron. 'Was she
amusing, President?' 'Yes, indeed, very amusing.' 'More so
than Mme du Deffand?' 'Oh, no, that would be saying too
much.' 'But which did you love the most?' 'Ha! I loved
Mme de Castelmoron!'

Mme du Deffand thought this exceedingly funny and
told everybody. She had another liaison, with Pont-de-
Veyle. Somebody once heard her say to him:

'Few attachments have lasted as long as ours—fifty years,
I should think?'

'More than fifty,' replied the old man.

'And all that time, not a cloud, not a cross word.'

'I shall always think how wonderful that is!' he said.

'But perhaps it is because we have really been rather
indifferent to each other?'

'Very possibly,' replied Pont-de-Veyle.

Mme de Deffand's most famous joke was the mot de

Saint Denis. Somebody was describing his martyrdom and how he walked from Paris to St Denis carrying his own head—five miles at least, was that not extraordinary? 'Dans une telle situation,' said Mme du Deffand, 'ce n'est que le premier pas qui coûte.'

It was not until she was quite middle-aged that her salon became famous. She was never rich, so she had no great house in which to entertain, but lived in a convent in the Rue St. Dominique (now the Ministry of War). 'Here,' said President Hénault, 'she gathered together a brilliant company; all deferred to her, she had a noble, generous heart. How many distinguished people would agree with this.' Indeed, her friends loved her even if she rather alarmed them. The charm of her salon lay in the mixture of the people to be found there: aristocrats, writers, politicians, philosophers, as well as any foreigner of note who happened to be visiting Paris. She liked to be surrounded by clever people in their party clothes and on their best behaviour, but she had no desire for intimacy. She used to say that supper was one of the four ends of man and that she had forgotten what the other three were. Her guests would begin to arrive at about six; supper was at half past nine. Mme du Deffand went to bed only when she could no longer induce anybody to sit up and talk with her. She lived for these evening hours of conversation and filled in the rest of the long day as best she could.

When Mme du Deffand was fifty-five a ghastly misfortune overtook her. She became blind. She accepted the affliction with the stoicism of her race and class: it is not considered polite in France to complain of the blows of fate. 'I am blind, Madame,' she wrote to her aunt, the Duchesse de Luynes. 'People praise my courage, but what would I

gain by despairing?' So little fuss did she make, in fact, that
her guests hardly realized that her sight was going. With
the horror of total blindness approaching, she decided to
have a change of air and went to stay with her brother, the
Comte de Vichy, on the family estate in Burgundy. Here
she found a Cinderella-like figure leading a miserable
existence, half servant, half poor relation, Julie de Lespinasse, Vichy's illegitimate daughter. Mme du Deffand took a
fancy to this lively girl of twenty, and when she went back
to Paris Julie went with her. She acted as secretary and
reader to her aunt and was an enormous asset to the *salon*;
everybody loved her and some fell in love with her, notably
the great d'Alembert, one of Mme du Deffand's most
regular guests.

For ten years the two women lived harmoniously, then
Mme du Deffand suddenly became aware that the most
brilliant members of her circle were in the habit of arriving
early and going for a gossip and a giggle to Julie's room
before turning up in the salon. Of course, by then they had
already told their good stories and fired off their jokes;
the cream had been skimmed from the milk. Mme du
Deffand's rage knew no bounds; Julie was sent packing.
But she did not go far. Her friends soon found her a flat in
the next street, the Rue de Bellechasse, and here she set up
a rival establishment, soon to become as famous as that of
her aunt. Parisians now had to choose between the two
ladies, because Mme du Deffand absolutely refused to
receive anybody who went to her niece. On the whole,
Julie took away the philosophic and progressive element
of society.

So strange is fate: both women are famous for their love
letters, classics of the French language. That Julie, young,

poor, and romantic, should have suffered from unrequited love was almost to be expected; that Mme du Deffand, at sixty-eight and stone blind, with her worldly wisdom and after the life she had led, should have caught the same complaint seems incredible. Yet so it was. The crotchety, cynical, spiteful, clever, worldly, witty son of a great father, Horace Walpole, twenty years younger than she, became the object of this unnatural and celebrated passion. Mlle de Lespinasse's love affair followed a more usual pattern. Her lover was an uninteresting young man named Guibert. He played fast and loose with her, married someone else, and yet never quite broke off his relationship with Julie. So here were the aunt and the niece, living only a few yards from each other, both suffering the tortures of the damned, dividing between them all the amusing elements of French society. Mme du Deffand never forgave, and when, in 1776 Julie died of a broken heart, she wrote without emotion: 'Mlle de Lespinasse died last night. Once this would have been an event in my life, but today it is nothing at all.'

The eighteenth-century salons—of which there were many, with Mme du Deffand's as the archetype—were temples dedicated to conversation. Only good talkers were admitted; the be-all and end-all of the evening was the cut and thrust of their encounters. If many of the guests were writers, that was because they had more to talk about than other people. Politicians as such were not sought after. One of Mme du Deffand's favourites was the Duc de Choiseul, who governed France for twelve years; but when he left his office desk behind him at Versailles, he had no desire to talk shop. Politics then were thought as dull as big business is now—in fact were always referred to as business: *les affaires*. But as the century drew to its revolutionary close, *les affaires* began to affect people's lives and therefore to interest everybody, and the salons became more and more political until they were a hotbed of intrigues and plots.

The heavy atmosphere of the nineteenth century, with its messages and meanings, its reforms, its scientific discoveries and German philosophy, fell like a wet blanket on the world, extinguishing the flame of pure pleasure which had hitherto burned so brightly and which has never been lit again. I do not think we should have cared to have been bossed by Mme de Staël, to have plotted at Mme Roland's, or to have drunk tea and eaten biscuits, Thackeray and Mrs Gaskell our fellow guests, at Mme Mohl's (born Mary Clarke); while heaven preserve us from such Sunday evenings as those of Marie d'Agoult, which she described as 'a burgeoning of youth'. The only nineteenth-century *salon* to compare for brilliant amusement with that of Mme du Deffand was presided over by Princesse Mathilde (1820–1904). Taine put his finger on the reason for her success. 'La politique achève de tuer le goût, l'aisance d'esprit, la sécurité de la conversation; vous leur gardez un asile.'

Mathilde Bonaparte was the daughter of Napoleon's youngest brother, Jerome, and Princess Catherine of Würtemberg, through whom she was closely related to the Czar of Russia and Queen Victoria. She took no account, however, of these royal relations, regarding herself as a Bonaparte, a Corsican; she positively worshipped the memory of Napoleon. 'The French Revolution,' she used to say, 'why, if it had never happened I should be selling oranges in the streets of Ajaccio! I am not one of those Princesses by divine right.' She was brought up in Rome;

after an early engagement to her cousin Louis Napoleon, which came to nothing, she was married off by her impecunious father to the richest man in Europe, Prince Demidov, who owned the Ural mines. He is always supposed to have been impossible and to have treated her like a brute, but in fact he had just cause for complaint. In St Petersburg he and his family were regarded as parvenus; when the newly married couple arrived at the Demidov palace Princesse Mathilde was invited to Court and to various aristocratic houses without her husband, a state of affairs to which she raised no objection. In any case her only desire was to live in Paris. Nothing pleased her in Russia, where Court life was stiff and dowdy, while the gipsies whom her husband frequented were dirty and dull. It was not easy to leave Russia, even in those days, and in spite of her friendship with her cousin the Czar, she was obliged to bribe her way out with jewels. 'Paris vaut bien des émeraudes,' she said. Her marriage came to an end, but the Czar saw to it that she had a huge settlement.

She set up house in the Rue de Courcelles, where she was surrounded by the most interesting men of the day. In spite of her name she never played at politics. When she first lived in Paris, Louis Philippe was on the throne. She was fond of him and his family, and, like Louis Napoleon's half-brother, the Duc de Morny, she was sorry when they were chased into exile. However, like the Duc de Morny, she had a favoured place under the Second Empire; indeed, until Louis Napoleon married, she acted as hostess for him. Understandably there was no love lost between her and Eugénie, and after the marriage Princesse Mathilde retired from Court. Soon she was receiving on a large scale at the Rue de Courcelles.

She dined every evening at seven-thirty with a few intimates; after dinner she was at home to the members of her circle. Her lover was Count Nieuwerkerke, curator of the Louvre, an excellent museum official but an odious man, a Don Juan, a dandy, and a rake, who treated her abominably and whom her other guests cordially disliked. He was always there, however, deferred to in everything. In 1860 she struck up a friendship with Sainte-Beuve. Soon he was presiding at her literary dinners which took place every Wednesday. By degrees, her salon, which had hitherto been composed of society people, became almost entirely literary. The Goncourt brothers, Taine, Renan, Mérimée, Dumas, Victor Hugo, Thiers, and in later years the young Proust and Heredia were regular guests. Flaubert read his *Education Sentimentale* aloud to her; she was one of the first to appreciate his genius. Gautier sat cross-legged at her feet like a Turk, until the horror of the modern world became too much for him and he died of melancholy in 1872. Certain writers, however, could not get on with her. Daudet went twice to the Rue de Courcelles, said the food was bad, and never returned. Musset went, but arrived an hour late, blind drunk, and was not asked again. George Sand went only once, on which occasion Gautier, Flaubert and the Goncourts showed off shamelessly. 'Ils sont bien bons,' said George Sand, 'ils ne me font pas le moindre effet.' Mathilde, on the whole, did not like women: 'If a woman comes into the room I have to change the conversation.'

The house in the Rue de Courcelles, which still exists and is much used now for charity bazaars, is typical of its date—huge and gloomy, with great drawing-rooms of bad proportions leading out of each other. Princesse Mathilde blanketed the walls with velvet draperies and covered them with second-rate pictures. Her conservatory was said to be like several junk shops in a virgin forest; even her contempories thought it awful. She herself was very much of her generation, though her natural and direct manner of speech sometimes startled the famous men around her. She had a strong—we should think exaggerated—family feeling, as people had in those days. Nobody was allowed to breathe a word against the Bonapartes. She quarrelled with Sainte-Beuve because he joined a newspaper where they were spoken of, she thought, unsuitably, and she argued with Sardou over his *Madame Sans-Gêne*. Taine sent her his *Origines de la France Contemporaine*, in which there is some mild criticism of Napoleon; she ordered her carriage and left a card at his house with 'P.P.C.' on it.

Just before the Second Empire fell Nieuwerkerke, feeling that Mathilde could be of no more use to him, left her. He had been so horrid to her for so long that his departure was more of a relief than a sorrow. She moved to a smaller house in the Rue de Berri, taking a young female companion to live there with her. A new lover appeared on the scene; the salon was more brilliant than ever and its hostess was considered to be one of the glories of the Third Republic. Alas, the companion fell into bed with the lover. 'La pauvre vieillarde amoureuse', as Taine called the Princess, was nearly seventy when she discovered their liaison; her Corsican temperament was as violent as ever and she was terribly unhappy; in spite of faithful friends who did everything they could think of to console her, her last years were darkened by this affair. She died in 1904, having played an important part in Parisian intellectual life for half a century.

Another half century has passed and the salon seems to have had its day. Society is too diffuse; people are too busy; manners have become too casual. If a hostess wished to indicate that somebody should not come back without a definite invitation, the usage was that she herself conducted him to the door. The intimates came and went quite casually. A modern hostess would find that few of her guests would take such a delicate hint. Where there were one or two foreign visitors to Paris, there are now a million. The French travel less than other people, but more than they used to. The essence of a salon is that its members are constantly together; they know each other so well that nothing has to be explained—they talk in a form of shorthand. With half of them away putting on plays in South America, lecturing in Athens, attending P.E.N. club meetings in Brussels, and so on, their intimacy would constantly be interrupted.

But perhaps when the atom bomb has cleared the air and when atomic energy has given back leisure to the world, there will once more be small gatherings of Frenchmen, looking like Hindu gods or Picasso paintings because of the fall-out, but none the less clever for that, ready to sit up all night with some brilliant and sympathetic hostess, enjoying the pleasures of repartee.

1961

Wicked Thoughts in Greece

THE visitor to Greece must not be put off by first impressions of Athens. It is probably the ugliest capital in Europe, worse, even, than Madrid, tying for horror with Moscow, which it resembles in that both are formless conglomerations of modern buildings overlooked by an immortal monument. Furthermore, it has a dreadful air of prosperous vulgarity which one does not expect to see this side of the Atlantic. The traffic is noisier, wilder, more evidently intent on homicide than that of Paris, and consists entirely of enormous pastel-coloured American motor-cars. Streets of new houses are going up everywhere, and one very inconvenient result of this is that nobody can tell you the way—neither taxi-drivers nor passers-by nor even the policemen know one street from another, everything is so new and uniform. And this hideous newness extends, in every direction, as far as the eye can see—Athens from the air is a desert of khaki-coloured cement.

I had the idea of walking up to the Parthenon instead of taking a cab; fortunately, because within a stone's throw of the hotel there is another world. A little old town, called the Plaka, covers the lower slopes of the Acropolis. It is very much like hundreds of Mediterranean hill-towns—Hyères, for instance—with narrow streets ending in flights of steps, houses washed in clear pale colours and roofed with Roman tiles, courtyards crammed with geraniums, pinks, orange and fig-trees; vines over everything, drains in the street—my first whiff of the south—the old ladies sitting beside them chatting their lives away.

The unique quality of the Plaka comes from the fact that round every corner there is some classical monument or fragment or Byzantine church, while overhead hangs the tremendous Parthenon. All is as Lord Byron must have seen it, though his hosts, the French monks, and their monastery have disappeared and fields of corn no longer wave between it and the Piraeus. Houses, churches, and monuments are on the right scale and at the right distance from each other, a rare and precious balance of which modern architects seldom take account. Alas! After ten minutes of happy wandering the dream is shattered and the dreadful wasteland of the Agora appears.

Here the American School of Classical Studies seems to have torn down whole streets in order to search for a few pots. Here the Americans are building, in a ghastly graveyard marble, the Stoa, said to be 'of Attalos', but really of Mr Homer A. Thompson. And here a gracious garden will be planted, complete, no doubt, with floral clock. This is only a beginning. The Greeks have been made to feel that the the Plaka is insanitary and (dread word) picturesque, an unworthy slum in a brave new capital city, and that it ought to go.

I went to see a learned English friend and found him sitting, like a Turkish lady, on his balcony. (Turkish ladies have their drawing-rooms built out at right-angles to the street so that they can see what goes on there.) His conversation was interspersed with remarks like: 'There's the yoghourt boy—late as usual. See that man with one leg?

'A little old town, called the Plaka . . .'

He's my plumber. I hope he's coming here. Oh well, another day no doubt.'

He said, 'Are you going to write about Greece?' 'I don't know,' I replied. 'Everybody is so kind to me and I'm having such a lovely time, and yet when I take up my pen my thoughts are wicked.' 'You must get out of Athens, or your thoughts will get wickeder and wickeder.' He was perfectly right, of course.

I visited one or two islands, and a learned American friend took me to Knossos, a fraudulent reconstruction like the Stoa, English this time, alas, and built in an *art nouveau* style reminiscent of Paris metro stations. It is evident that Anglo-Saxons should be kept away from Mediterranean sites; French and German archaeologists never make these dreadful errors of taste. Knossos, however, matters less than the Stoa, because it is out in the country and does not spoil anything else. The Stoa in all its vileness hits the eye from the Acropolis and the Temple of Hephaestus. It is as though the French had allowed Frank Lloyd Wright to build his idea of a Petit Trianon at the bottom of the *tapis vert* at Versailles. Apart from Knossos, I greatly enjoyed three days in Crete and had the agreeable experience of meeting one of Paddy Leigh Fermor's partisans in a bus. He was treating Paddy's book, with a photograph of himself, rather like a passport, bringing it out on every occasion. Finally I hired a motor-car and went with my learned American for a tour of the Peloponnese, returning by Delphi. Only then did I understand the real point and greatness of Greece.

We know that Greece is beautiful, just as we know that Heaven is, but knowing is not the same as seeing. Photographs are not much help. The works of man are thin on the ground compared with any other civilized country—indeed, my learned English friend in Athens greeted me with the words, 'There is nothing to see here, you know'—but man himself is splendidly in harmony with a splendid land.

The Peloponnese has many different sorts of scenery: it can resemble Provence, Tuscany, and even Scotland, each at its very best, and it is inhabited by a race of beauties. It breathes the prosperity, real, solid and eternal, which comes from hard work on fertile soil, very different from the meretricious prosperity of Athens, based on the whimsical dollar. I liked to see the people living on such good terms with their beasts. The roads, where motors hardly ever appear, are covered with mules and goats and cows; my little chauffeur drove with great consideration and never once made a baby donkey jump or an old lady run for dear life.

We went first to Eleusis: still under the dead hand of Athens, it sits in a cement factory; no magic here. Then to Nauplia for a swim, and then Mycenae. 'Great God, this is an awful place.' And haunted. If Miss Jourdain and Miss Moberley had come here instead of that other palace at Versailles they might have had An Adventure indeed. The golden treasure, by the way, is no longer shown to the public, but lies buried in the Bank of Greece. Was it for this that Frau Schliemann, surrounded by armed troops, worked with her penknife day and night for three weeks, robbing the ancient dead? Here, at Olympia and at Delphi the excavations have all been carried out in perfect taste; the ruins lie in their own wonderful background and tell their own wonderful story. The museums are a model; the hotels, even, are not horrible to look at.

Perhaps best of everything I liked Hosios Loukas, the Byzantine church in its almond grove on a mountainside, still tended, as it has been for nearly a thousand years, by the monks of its own monastery. Unspoilt both inside and out, with its incomparable mosaics and brickwork, Hosios Loukas gives the happy, holy feeling of a great work of art. Mercifully, it is very far from Athens. We must hope that Mr Homer A. Thompson will never get there.

Back in Athens for a last dinner-party with a learned Greek friend whom I am obliged to call the Desecrator, because he goes round the country removing '*bon dieu-series*' from churches. He does it with the purest intentions and in the interests of good taste. But I believe Byzantine churches are meant to be filled with holy clutter: if you take away the eikons and put them in museums or the Desecrator's dining-room and throw away the little images beloved of the peasants, the Bon Dieu himself flies out of the windows. However, I can forgive the Desecrator a great deal on account of his dinners. Abler pens than mine have described the horrors of Greek food (in the country places one is obliged to exist on bread and water, both excellent). But Greece is not a country of happy mediums: everything there seems to be either wonderful or horrible, and my friend's food is wonderful. It is worth the voyage from Paris to dine with him; his cook must be one of the best in Europe.

1955

In Defence of Louis XV

DR GOOCH is one of our most revered historians, but he is
not interested in human beings. Occupied with historical
trends and political events, he sees the characters concerned
in them as the stereotyped heroes and villains of a fairy
story: the Great King, the Bad King, the Good Prince (who
always, alas, dies young), and Princess Charming. In his
Life of Louis XV he describes that complicated freak Louis
XIII as colourless. He sees the Duchesse de Bourgogne as a
sort of female Lord Fauntleroy, the darling of the Great
King's heart; no mention of her ugliness, her orgies of
eating and drinking, her lovers, the fact that, like Marie-
Antoinette, she constantly sent State secrets to her own
relations when they were fighting the French, and her dis-
concerting habit of having an enema in front of the drawing-
room fire before dinner. All who knew her adored her in
spite of her faults and oddities, and therein lies her interest;
to Dr Gooch she is simply the Rose of Savoy. Her husband
was a Good Prince and they both died young, greatly
regretted by Dr Gooch. But this Good Prince had the faults
of his virtues. He was very bigoted. His son Louis XV is
blamed for persecuting the *philosophes*—would Bourgogne
have persecuted them less? Another Good Prince who died
young, also regretted by Dr Gooch, was the 'Polish
Dauphin', the son of Louis XV, who thought that Voltaire

should be tortured to death. Had he come to the throne there might have been some very odd goings-on.

Dr Gooch's theme and subtitle is Monarchy in Decline. Now, we all like to give the French Revolution a single author. 'Voltaire a fait tout ce que nous voyons,' said Condorcet in 1793. 'Infâme Pitt, c'était ton ouvrage,' cried Soulavie. Nobody knows better than Dr Gooch the responsibilities of Marie-Antoinette in this matter. But she is a Princess Charming and must not be scolded, so he points his accusing finger at the Bad King, Louis XV. Please, Sir, may I speak? Surely if any one person was to blame it was the Great King, Louis XIV. He died leaving France more ruined than ever in her history, the country one enormous hospital. He eliminated the admirable Huguenots. He separated the King of France from his subjects and the nobles from their domains, and knitted up a political tangle which could never be unravelled and which finally had to be cut by the guillotine.

However, Dr Gooch very much prefers him to Louis XV, who would not 'mend his ways'. What were his ways? He was merciful, 'too weak to punish', and wished for peace, 'too easy-going'. He lacked self-confidence and left important decisions to his Ministers. (He would have been a good constitutional monarch had the Great King seen fit to leave any sort of constitution.) He is reproached for laziness; this is simply unfair. He got up at five o'clock every morning, lighting his own fire in the winter, in order to get through the work on hand. He had a series of incompetent ministers —this may or may not have been his fault. The politicians, like the generals of his reign, were a poor lot. Cut off as he was, by the Great King's dispositions, from the life of his capital, it is difficult to know how he should have set about making the clean sweep which alone would have been of any use. Dr Gooch hardly mentions the work he was doing with Maupeou which was interrupted by the King's death and the Chancellor's dismissal, yet some historians think that had it been achieved the course of events would have been very different.

What Dr Gooch cannot forgive is his love of pleasure. Surely a King who loves pleasure is less dangerous than one who loves glory? It should be remembered, too, that in the eighteenth century pleasure was not regarded with the cold disapproval of our dismal age. Helvétius thought it was the ultimate good; even Frederick the Great said it was the truest reality of our existence. It would have been very strange had Louis XV felt like the Prince Consort about pleasure. Dr Gooch also furiously takes him to task for loving women. Oddly enough, some men do.

Most of the facts marshalled against Louis XV in this book come from the memoirs of disgruntled Ministers. But memoirs are not always reliable evidence, as everybody knows who has reached an age when contemporaries are writing them. Dr Gooch is inclined to quote only from those which prove his case. (Mme de Pompadour's letter on the Calas affair: le bon coeur du roi a bien souffert au récit de cette étrange aventure et toute la France crie vengeance is, of course, ignored.) He takes the death-bed scene from Liancourt, who says that the King's cowardice was beyond description, rather than from Cröy, who says the exact opposite. But the Bad King must come to a Bad End, to serve him right for having had a Good Time.

1956

Chic—English, French and American

I REALLY prefer the word elegance. 'Chic' has lost value in its native country—'Chic alors!' cries the street urchin on finding ten francs in the gutter—and it never had much prestige in England. Roget in his *Thesaurus* lumps it together with 'style, swank, swagger and showing off'; indeed, it represents everything that the English most dislike, a sort of bright up-to-date fashionableness they have never aspired to. For elegance in England is of such different stuff from that in any other country that it is not easy to make foreigners believe in it at all. (As regards the women, that is. English men and small children are universally admitted to be the model of good dressing; our Queen and Princess Margaret set the fashion for the world until they were ten.) It is based upon a contempt of the current mode and a limitless self-assurance.

When the Empress Eugénie paid a state visit to England she went with Queen Victoria to the opera. The Londoners sighed a little as the two ladies stood together in the Royal Box during the playing of the National Anthem; the beauty in her Paris clothes beside chubby little red-faced Victoria. Then the time came for them to take their seats. The Empress, with a graceful movement, looked round at her chair, but Queen Victoria dumped straight down, thus proving unmistakably that she was of Royal birth and

106

'The Empress, with a graceful movement, looked round at her chair,
but Queen Victoria dumped straight down. . . .'

upbringing. Had that chair not been in its place the skies would have fallen, and she knew it. The audience was proud of its Queen and never gave the parvenue Empress another thought—indeed, nobody in England was at all surprised when shortly afterwards the Second Empire collapsed.

Nearer our own time two English duchesses were turned away from Christian Dior. The people at the entrance considered them too dowdy to be admitted. In England, if you are a duchess you don't need to be well dressed—it would be thought quite eccentric. I cannot imagine why they ever had the idea of going to Dior, where they would certainly not have ordered anything. Perhaps they were tired after extensive sight-seeing and thought they would like to sit for a while, having a vision of Monsieur Worth's soothing empty salons in the days when their mothers dressed there. (In the days of their grandmothers Monsieur Worth came to the house like any other tradesman.) They had surely not envisaged the scented scramble at the top of the stairs, the enervating atmosphere of a salon where no window may ever be opened, the hideous trellis of crossed nylon legs round the room, and the all-in wrestling match for each and every chair. The duchesses went quietly, and if they did not quite realize what an escape they had had, they were probably rather happy to sit on a bench in the Avenue Montaigne and watch the motors go by.

At the beginning of this century the English were rich and pleasure-loving; foreign currency was no problem; society women bought all their clothes in Paris. When the dresses were delivered they were put away for at least two years, since, in those days, nothing was considered so common as to be dressed in the height of fashion. Harlots and actresses could flaunt the current clothes, it was quite all right for them, and indeed a mark of their profession, but 'one of us, dear child', never. Even the men would not think of wearing a new suit until it had spent one or two nights in the garden, making it look at least a year old.

Now this tradition continues in London. The dress-makers there slavishly follow the Paris fashion of two years before, while people in the streets lag another year, so that to anybody arriving from Paris the clothes have an odd and disproportioned look, skirts too long or short, waists too high or too low, and so on. Anyhow, the word elegant cannot truthfully be applied to the English by day. Ladylike is the most that can be said. They really have no idea of what day-clothes should be; and contrary to what is some-times supposed, their sports and country clothes are de-plorable. They are of tweed thick and hard as a board, in various shades of porridge, and made to last for ever. For the town English women have only one solution, a jacket and tight skirt with what the fashion papers call 'a cunning slit up the back', which, when they walk, divides rather horribly over their calves.

Women seen about in London streets give a general appearance of tidy dreariness, but these same women at a ball are a surprise and a delight. In the evening they excel. With their beautiful jewels glittering on their beautiful skins, with their absolute unself-consciousness, put them in any old satin skirt and deep décolleté and they are unbeat-able. There is no more dazzling sight than a ball at Bucking-ham Palace.

French women, we are often told, are the most elegant. But where are they? Foreigners visiting Paris for the first time are often disappointed because they never see anybody well dressed. The fact is that elegance in Paris is confined to a small group of women who are seldom seen in public and never in the streets. They get into their own motors inside their own courtyards, rarely eat in restaurants or appear at the big dressmakers' (a selection of the clothes is sent for them to see at home), and in short it is an act of faith for the ordinary tourist to believe that they exist at all. They do, however, and are absolutely powerful in the world of elegance, since it is their taste which, in the end, everybody follows.

French dress designers, hairdressers, and cooks are admitted to be unbeatable, but they lose their eye, their hand, their skill after a few years in England or America. Why? Because they are no longer under the disciplinary control of les femmes du monde—that is to say, of a very few rich, ruthless, and savagely energetic women who know what they want and never spare anybody's feelings in their determination to get it. Back goes the dress, back goes the dish, back into the washtub goes the head, until the result is perfect—then and then only is heard the grudging 'Pas mal'. Their vigilance extends to the smallest details. I once bought a suit in an expensive English shop and gave it to my Paris dressmaker for some minor alteration. She told me she had been obliged to take it home and do it herself, since she could not risk letting the girls in her workroom see how badly it was finished off. 'But how could you have accepted it?' she kept saying. I didn't like to tell her that I had not turned it inside out, as any French woman would have done, so had no idea how the seams were sewn.

Anglo-Saxons do not quite understand French elegance and what it is. They have a vague romantic notion that any French woman can take any old bit of stuff, give it a clever twist, and look chic in it. This may be true of Italian peasants, but not of Parisians. Dressing, in Paris, is not a craft; it is an art not to be come by easily or cheaply; Parisians are not peasants, but citizens of the most civilized town in the world. When they cannot afford the time and money to be really well dressed, they abandon the idea of clothes and concentrate instead upon cooking and their children's education. Dresses with a cheaply fashionable air do not appeal to French women.

In writing about Americans I find myself at a disadvantage so great that perhaps I really should not attempt it. For I have never been to America. I study it, of course. I look at *Life* and *Time* and the *New Yorker*; I hang about behind Americans at cocktail parties and listen to what they are saying to each other. I read their books, in many of which they seem to behave oddly, nipping off their own breasts with garden shears and so on, but no more oddly I suppose than the English of *Wuthering Heights*. America is to me some great star observed through a telescope, and I never feel quite sure that it exists, now, or whether its light is not coming to me across centuries of time (future time, of course).

If I may venture then to speak about American elegance, as observed through my telescope during many a long wakeful night, I should say it is the elegance of adolescence. The bobby-soxers, the teen-agers, who seem to what we call 'come out' so very young, are beautifully dressed. Their neat little clothes have more than an echo of Paris; the skirts are the right length, the waists in the right place, and they are, very suitably for children, understated. I imagine it would not do to turn them inside out and examine the seams. These young Americans do not care to have one good dress and wear it a whole season; they would rather have a quantity of cheap dresses and throw them away after two or three wearings. As I look through my telescope I see a charming flock of radiant little girls, in pretty dolls' clothes, clean, shining, with regular if rather big, teeth, wonderful figures and china skins. I also see a crowd of gracious ladies in canasta gowns, impeccable, not one blue hair out of place. But what happens to the intermediate ages? At what point do old little girls turn into young old ladies? Where are the grown-up women in the prime of life dressed as adults?

I think that the elegance of these three countries can be summed up by saying that in England the women are elegant until they are ten years old and perfect on grand occasions; in France a few women are entirely elegant always; in America most women are smart and impeccable, but with too much of an accent on immaturity for real elegance. The Latin American woman dressed in Paris is the very height of perfection, however.

1951

The Other Island

IRELAND has changed its name to Eire and its charming
people, whose qualities of heart and mind were so cruelly
misused for so many centuries, are busily making a nation,
but it is still the Emerald Isle of nineteenth-century literature, exaggeratedly itself. I go there every spring to stay
with various friends; my spirits rise with my body as the
little Aer Lingus plane flaps away from Le Bourget like an
owl. It is well named Friend Ship; whereas other airlines
are beginning to follow the horrid maxim of B.E.A. 'do not
spoil the passengers', the Friend Ship is organized to please.
There is a delicious luncheon of hot soup, fresh salmon and
hot coffee, after which the passengers settle down to enjoy
the soothing headlines of *The Irish Times* and *The Cork
Examiner*: 'Dublin Nun Found Dead in Drain', 'Priest
Hurt in Collision with Cart', 'Departing Nuncio's Tribute
to Ireland'. The new, restless Europe is already far away.
The Friend Ship's wings are above the cabin so that one
can see out as from a helicopter. England is a jewel wrapped
in cotton wool, but over the Irish Channel a blue horizon
glimmers and in it lies the dark green velvet land. A
cold sun shines on the fields; they are dotted with small
houses like the ancestral home of President Kennedy,
that white-washed box with two tiny windows which has
figured on many a Christmas card. The Irish are naturally

proud of this local boy who has made so very good.

There is an hour or two to spend in Dublin before catching a train to the south. It is a prim little eighteenth-century town, sometimes compared to Bath, though this is doing it too much honour; and unspoilt. So, come to think of it, are most capital cities in Western Europe—hard to name another that has suffered like our poor London. (How can a rich and civilized race, devoted to its own history, have come to allow such destruction? Once a charming city, London is now a heap of rubbishy jerry buildings. No wonder the young citizens march about and sit down proclaiming that they do not want it to be defended and have no intention of dying for it.)

A little wait at Dublin station, time enough to write one's name in tin for a penny and weigh oneself for another. The May wind is bitter. Some American women are shivering on a bench, huddled in their plastic cloaks. One of them goes to the refreshment-room in search of hot coffee—comes back and says: 'Don't go in there, it's just dismal.' The train is an omnibus. Four nuns make a quick dash to instal themselves by the four front windows, which they open. The wind rushes in; it beats on the plastic garments of the Americans and disturbs their hair nets; they suffer for a while and then one of them goes forward: 'Pourdon me, could you close the windows?' But the nuns, in their veiling and mens' boots are feeling the heat; they observe custody of the eyes and pretend not to have heard. If the temperature totters into the forties the Irish, as it were, reach for their solar topees. There are many farmers in the train who have been to an agricultural show; they, too, are feeling the heat, there are sighs and groans and mopping of brows. They scrape manure off their trousers with knives and talk like an Abbey Theatre play. 'I've had another anonymous letter from Dooley O'Sullivan.' Delicious dinner of bacon and eggs and then we arrive at Limerick Junction. The cold sun is still shining, though it is now half past nine.

The plain of Tipperary is the richest farm land in Western Europe, so fertile that farming there requires little skill; beasts are simply left in the fields until they are fat enough to be sold. It is beautiful beyond words and empty. People leave Eire as they have always left Ireland, at an enormous rate. Every village, however small and poor, has a luggage shop. The plan on which the villages are built, one long, immensely wide street which can be used as a market, bordered by tiny houses, accentuates their emptiness. The admirable roads are bare of traffic—for miles and miles there is nothing except, occasionally, an enormous man spanking along in a donkey cart or a Rolls-Royce with American tourists buried in white satin luggage. The cottagers' dogs are so unused to motor traffic that they crouch and spring dangerously at passing cars. The green deserted fields lying beneath blue deserted mountains; the windowless mills dripping with creepers; the towers for captive princesses inhabited by owl and raven; the endless walls surrounding ghostly demesnes, the lodge gates, rusted up and leading into hay; the roofless churches, with elegant neo-Gothic spires rising out of nettle-beds make a melancholy but enchanted impression. Everywhere are nettles and those black birds, rooks, crows, ravens, jackdaws, which, in France, are indiscriminately known as *corbeaux*.

Historians of England record with surprise that Anglo-Saxons were never known to dwell in Roman villas left vacant by the fall of the Empire and the departure of their owners. The villas were solidly built of stone with such conveniences as central heating and baths, but the natives preferred to live out their short and brutish lives in horrid little wooden or wattle huts. This situation is strangely repeated today in Eire. What was good enough for President Kennedy's ancestors is good enough for the Irish. Within a stone's throw of their cabins there may be a great beautiful house deserted by its owners during the Troubled Times, positively inviting tenants. Why does not the whole village move in—plenty of room for everybody? But it remains empty. Eventually such houses are pronounced unsafe and blown up with gunpowder; sometimes the stones 'go on the roads', but often they lie in great heaps on the beautiful sites (walled or terraced gardens, lakes, avenues, carefully planted arboreta), monuments to the oddity of mankind. The Irish Government is not interested in 'ascendancy architecture' and would exchange any amount of Wyatt houses against one Celtic cross.

Those of the Anglo-Irish who have held on to their places are now happy in them again. An occasional reminder of the civil war, such as machine-gun marks in the nursery passage, framed, with the date, is only the relic of an historical past. If the Irish still hate us they show no signs of it, beyond an understandable gloating when President Kennedy turns the screw. Country house life resembles the French vie de château more than the quick weekend dash of the English. As in France, small unfortified country houses are called Castle. Guests move in for a good long stay, with their dogs, children, embroidery and fishing-rods. There is generally an invalid to be tenderly inquired for. 'She was wandering this afternoon and then went into such a very sound sleep that I sent for the doctor. He hopes that next time the chemist won't muddle up the labels.' A couple is

invited from another part of Ireland; they reply by telegram:
'Bother arrive by car Tuesday.' 'If it's such a bother—'
says the hostess crossly until she realizes that the word
should be both.

The houses are beautiful in their provincial way and
have such romantic names as Ann's Grove, Dereen,
Newtown Anner. They are full of treasures (with the oddest
attributions, like *Madame du Barry by Largilliere*) in a
hotch potch of rubbish. The china cabinet will contain Rose
Pompadour Sèvres cheek by jowl with A Present from
Bexhill; old *Tatlers* in a bookshelf are muddled up with
Oudry's *Fables de La Fontaine*. All this is a happy hunting-
ground for dishonest dealers. The famous Irish plaster work
is often coarse and rather ugly, too much like the plaster in
which somebody's leg has recovered from a Swiss accident
stuck on the wall. French gardening amateurs, who arrived
in a bus, annoyed one of my hostesses by exclaiming:
'Comme c'est charmant, tout ce désordre britannique!'

There is still a feudal flavour about domestic life, for
servants abound, and delightful they are. The kitchen teems
with scullions and the servants' hall nourishes many more
people than actually work in the house. The atmosphere
below stairs is jolly; quarrels are rare. Food is of paramount
importance and the houses vie with each other to delight
the guests. It is rather too rich for me, based on cream.
A typical Irish dinner would be: cream flavoured with
lobster, cream with bits of veal in it, green peas and cream,
cream cheese, cream flavoured with strawberries. I crave
skim milk from an English coalmine, but then I have not
been on the river all day to sharpen my appetite. Sometimes
we lunch, on cold cream, in the fishing-hut. There is a
sheaf of telegraph forms hanging up in case somebody feels

like having a bet, when a boy on a pony is sent off to the nearest post office.

The village is a splendid shopping centre. It has not yet got a boutique (pronounced bowtike), like Clonmel, but the draper, whose white china horse in the window proclaims him to be a Protestant, has a range of lovely cotton dresses for 12s. 6d., and I stock up with his nylons for the whole year. Medical Hall keeps French cosmetics and scent. Next door to where it says 'Yoke your Team to a Pierce Machine' there is an exciting new notice: Modern Hairstyling. I ask about it in Medical Hall. Oh yes, there are two young ladies trained at New York and they wash your hair backwards. The young ládies have already lost some of the transatlantic hustle, I note. It is half past eleven when I ring their bell; the receptionist is still in her dressing-gown. However, my hair is beautifully washed and the bill is 6s.

The Troubled Times are wonderfully over, but can never be forgotten. Their history is that of all resistance movements, ruthless and terrible, with internal factions and betrayals that engendered the blackest hatreds.

> 'Twas the twenty-eighth day of November
> Outside of the town of Macroon
> The Tans in their big Crossley tender
> Were hurtling along to their doom.
> The lads in the column were waiting
> Their hand grenades primed, on the spot,
> And the Irish Republican Army
> Made balls of the whole fucking lot.

It seems strange that the kindly, gentle, rather lazy Irish

should have been the first to prove that in our modern communities violence always pays. The nation which now comes into being after such revolutionary birth throes, has some unexpected features. It is prim like Dublin architecture; it submits to Rome; it is old-fashioned. When *The Irish Times* publishes the titles of current successful novels, including at least one book which has been warmly praised by Catholic writers in other lands, it is not 'for holiday reading'; it is a list of the books banned in Eire on moral grounds. In the same issue a letter from Mr John Moore complains that a novel of his, which *The Irish Times* itself has described as 'unremittingly pleasant' and which has been read out on the English wireless as A Book at Bedtime, is on the list.

The piety of the Irish has often been turned to patriotic ends and still has a nationalistic flavour. To this day there is not much fraternization with Protestants. I asked my hostess what would happen if she asked the priest to dinner. 'If he came,' she said, 'he would very soon be moved to another parish.' A pagan element, too, remains and it is sometimes difficult to know whether saints are being honoured or the Little People. Rags tied to thorn bushes are said to be for the latter, but they look like the ribbons which French peasants tie on the Virgin and the thorn tree surely has a Christian association. I would like to hear more of the Little People, but nobody talks about them very much and they seem to have gone underground. The barrows and prehistoric earthworks still may not be excavated for fear of disturbing them. I asked an old keeper, but he had only seen their pipes—when I looked disappointed he said: 'I saw a sow where never a sow there was,' and that was the nearest I have ever got to them. There is said to be a fairy's shoe in the Dublin museum. It was found in a bog and the fact that it is worn out proves it is not a doll's shoe.

The rulers of Eire want the people to speak Irish. It is taught in the schools as a second language; all official notices and forms are written in it, with an English crib. It is really rather easy, the sort of language one could invent oneself. *Corneal* = corner, *telefon* = telephone, *aerphort* = airport, etc. But parents do not approve of their children being made to waste time learning Irish at *scoil* and there is a good deal of resistance to it. Some Common Market language would certainly be more useful. In fact, Eire does not live with the times. Before the English ascendancy Ireland ignored 'the new restless Europe with its Crusades and Hildebrandine movements, its stone castles, cathedrals, its feudalism, its charters, its trade routes and all the stir of modernity',[1] and now that the ascendancy is over she turns her back on the atomic age.

It might be easier to foresee the future of Ireland if one knew the inwardness of her past. She has had no Michelet, no Trevelyan, of her own. Perhaps historiography is not an Irish talent; an Englishman might well find the close scrutiny of his own ancestors at their very worst rather depressing. For reasons of space, historians of England can only present this strange people, in its fairy-like island, as John Bull's worrying neighbour; this is not good enough. Some young genius ought now to begin his life's work, a great History of Ireland.

1962

[1] G. M. Trevelyan.

The Tourist

'FOREIGNER, differing from speaker in language and customs, outside the Roman Empire; rude, wild, or uncultured person.' The Barbarian of yesterday is the Tourist of today and he still preys on the rich old cities where our civilization began.

A horde of displaced persons on the move throughout the summer months is one of the features, one of the problems of our age. What is the meaning of this yearly migration? Why do hundreds of thousands of human beings feel impelled to leave comfortable establishments for the certain misery of the voyage and the uncertain amenities of the arrival, not to speak of danger to life and limb? Americans see typhoid germs wickedly lurking in every drop of European water and regard Europe as a dreaded smallpox area. There are the hazards of ship, aeroplane, and motor-coach. The last named has a way of taking to the air from mountain roads and being pulverized at level crossings, so that neither hill nor plain can be considered perfectly safe. All tourists half expect to be murdered. So it is brave as well as energetic of them to tour. Why do they do it?

The answer is that the modern dwelling is comfortable, convenient, and clean, but it is not a home. Now that people live on shelves, perched between earth and sky, with nowhere to sit out of doors, no garden where they can plant a flower or pick a herb, they are driven on to the road for their holidays. All human beings need some aesthetic nourishment and the inhabitants of ugly towns form the bulk of the tourist trade. A search for beauty, known as sight-seeing, is common to all tourists; as well as that, each nationality has a particular incentive to travel.

The English are a restless island race, fond of moving about, and the Grand Tour is an old tradition with them. The French from the north are in search of sunshine, the meridional French, like Latin Americans, have light, beauty and civilization at home, they need not move and seldom do. The North Americans very naturally want to get away from North America. They are also after their own origins. Although they descend from people who could not succeed in Europe and furiously shook its dust from their feet, they have a sentimental feeling for ancestors. They even look for them in England, nurturing a strange belief that in some country churchyard Hoggefeller and Potemkine lie dust to dust with Hogward and Potkin. They also come to shop. Tired of mass-produced, synthetic materials, looking like the froth from detergents, which choke up the Fifth Avenue emporiums, they feel a need for real lace and linen, anything hand-made, even baskets: 'Look,' I said to an American woman beside me in an aeroplane over Florence, 'that is the Duomo.' She replied: 'Until what time do the stores remain open here?'

The Germans are a different matter. They make straight for the rich lands they have always coveted and never conquered; they clank about in imaginary armour, marching, shouting, occupying. They take a more intelligent interest in what they see than the other tourists do, and they long to own it all. Probably, now, they never will; but they frighten me.

It cannot be said that these modern barbarians do much harm. They do not sack or rape or plunder or pillage, raze to the ground or sow with salt; they pay, rather grudgingly sometimes, for what they take. They no longer carve their names on famous statues or chip off bits of mosaic for souvenirs. Their breath is not good for pictures, but that is not their fault. The worst thing they have done, to a classical site, is the erection of the Stoa. Some Americans, who had probably seen the Victor Emmanuel monument on their way through Rome, generously decided to present the Athenians with its equivalent which they call the Stoa of Attalos. It is ghastly, but does not matter much, since Athens is past praying for. The Greeks themselves have torn down the charming city which we know from old prints (a Sick Man or two prettily fezzed in the foreground), which Lord Byron loved, and which cannot have been so very different, in its ageless Mediterranean way, from that which Socrates saw. They have replaced it with a formless mass of concrete which has even crept on to the Acropolis itself. We cannot blame the tourists for that. Nor are they to be blamed if, as too often happens in Italy, their hosts, anxious to accommodate them comfortably, pull down the architecture they have come to see and put up that from which they are running away.

I have observed the tourist at close quarters in Paris, Versailles, and the Venetian lagoon. No, reader, I am not one myself. I am far too lazy to rush about seeing things. As I live in Paris I have no need to go elsewhere for shopping or to satisfy my aesthetic appetite. However I cannot work at

home. I have stayed at Versailles and Torcello when writing
books. I go every year to Venice as a visitor, not a tourist;
there is a world of difference between the two. (The tourist
tours, he seldom spends a week in the same place. The visitor
stops in a town and leads the life of its inhabitants.)

Paris is a capital city and the foreigner there makes little
impact, except at Easter, when what the papers call *une
pluie d'Anglais* falls on it. Thousands of cheerful young
people come over for two or three days, sun themselves,
after a long dark winter, at café tables on the pavements
and exude a great deal of jollity. I often think what a funny
Paris they find, empty, with no shops or theatres open,
many of the best restaurants closed and half the windows shut-
tered. Very different from the town which its inhabitants
know!

Both Versailles and Venice can swallow up enormous
crowds; they need them, perhaps, to keep the ghosts at bay.
Versailles has been open to the public ever since it was
built; Venice too has always been thronged with visitors
from East and West. It is saved by its situation from the one
disfigurement with which the modern tourist can fairly
be reproached, the parked motor-car; at Versailles the
gardens and the view from the terrace are also free from
that. Trianon, alas, is smothered in the dirty tin boxes,
like a flower beneath a swarm of flies.

One thing about tourists is that it is very easy to get away
from them. Like ants they follow a trail and a few yards
each side of that trail there are none. In Paris they keep to
the shopping centres and Saint Germain-des-Prés. I have
never seen one where I live, less than a mile south of the
river. At Versailles the trail is even narrower. There is an
excellent tea shop, one of those pretty nineteenth-century

'I have observed the tourist at close quarters. . . .'

bakeries with stucco ceiling and wall paintings where you can sit down and drink a cup of chocolate with your croissant. It is perhaps three minutes' walk from where the motor-coaches park, but no tourists ever find it and its brisk trade depends entirely on local widows. Nobody visits the eighteenth-century Théâtre Montausier, the library (one of the most beautiful in the world) or the Musée Houdon. These things are just off the trail. People are exhausted after visiting the château and have no energy left for the town.

In Venice, the side canals, most of the churches except St Mark's, most of the museums except the Accademia are empty and peaceful. The country everywhere, ten yards from a main road, is safe, since tourists on the whole are uninterested in scenery and anyhow in a hurry to get on. Part of their enjoyment lies in describing their tour to people at home; the evocation of a French wood of straight white poplars which seem to be waiting for a unicorn; of the melancholy pale-green Veneto; of the rich and varied Peloponnese would not amuse the neighbours. The tourist confines himself to famous bricks and mortar in front of which he can photograph his wife and Junior. (Oh! must he bring Junior? Need he? I love children, especially when they cry, because then somebody takes them away. But Junior can yell his head off and nobody takes him away. Is it good for him to travel? Does he enjoy it? Why not leave him at home?)

The most intensive study I ever made of tourists was at Torcello, where it is impossible to avoid them. Torcello is a minute island in the Venetian lagoon: here, among vineyards and wild flowers, some thirty cottages surround a great cathedral which was being built when William the

Conqueror came to England. A canal and a path lead from
the lagoon to the village; the vineyards are intersected by
canals; red and yellow sails glide slowly through the vines.
Bells from the campanile ring out reproaches three times a
day ('*cloches, cloches, divins reproches*') joined by a chorus
from the surrounding islands. There is an inn where I
lived one summer, writing my book and observing the
tourists. Torcello which used to be lonely as a cloud has
recently become an outing from Venice. Many more visitors
than it can comfortably hold pour into it, off the regular
steamers, off chartered motor-boats, and off yachts; all
day they amble up the tow-path, looking for what? The
cathedral is decorated with early mosaics—scenes from
hell, much restored, and a great sad, austere Madonna;
Byzantine art is an acquired taste and probably not one in
ten of the visitors has acquired it. They wander into the
church and look round aimlessly. They come out on to the
village green and photograph each other in a stone arm-
chair, said to be the throne of Attila. They relentlessly
tear at the wild roses which one has seen in bud and longed
to see in bloom and which, for a day have scented the
whole island. As soon as they are picked the roses fade
and are thrown into the canal. The Americans visit the
inn to eat or drink something. The English declare that
they can't afford to do this. They take food which they
have brought with them into the vineyard and I am sorry to
say leave the devil of a mess behind them. Every Thursday
Germans come up the tow-path, marching as to war, with
a Leader. There is a standing order for fifty luncheons
at the inn; while they eat the Leader lectures them through
a megaphone. After luncheon they march into the cathedral
and undergo another lecture. They, at least, know what

they are seeing. Then they march back to their boat. They are tidy; they leave no litter.

More interesting, however, than the behaviour of the tourists is that of the islanders. As they are obliged, whether they like it or not, to live in public during the whole summer, they very naturally try to extract some financial benefit from this state of affairs. The Italian is a born actor; between the first boat from Venice, at 11 a.m. and the last on which the ordinary tourist leaves at 6 p.m., the island is turned into a stage with all the natives playing a part. Young men from Burano, the next island, dress up as gondoliers and ferry tourists from the steamer to the village in sandolos. One of them brings a dreadful little brother called Eric who pesters everybody to buy the dead bodies of sea-horses, painted gold. 'Buona fortuna', he chants. I got very fond of Eric. Sweet-faced old women sit at the cottage doors selling postcards and trinkets and apparently making *point de Venise* lace. They have really got it, on sale or return, from relations in Burano, where it is made by young girls. Old women, with toil-worn hands, cannot do such fine work. It is supposed that the tourists are more likely to buy if they think they see the lace being made, but hardly any of them seem to appreciate its marvellous quality. Babies toddle about offering four-leafed clovers and hoping for a tip. More cries of 'Buona fortuna'. The priest organizes holy processions to coincide with the arrival of the steamer. And so the play goes on. The tourists are almost incredibly mean, they hardly leave anything on the island except empty cigarette boxes and flapping *Daily Mails*. The lace is expensive, but they might buy a few postcards or shell necklaces and give the children some pennies; they seem to have hearts of stone.

As soon as the last boat has gone, down comes the curtain. The 'gondoliers' shed their white linen jackets and silly straw hats and go back to Burano, taking Eric, highly dissatisfied with his earnings and saying if this goes on he will die of hunger. The sweet old women let the smiles fade from their faces, put away their lace-making pillows, and turn to ordinary activities of village life such as drowning kittens. The father of the clover babies creeps about on his knees finding four-leafed clovers for the next day. The evening reproaches ring out, the moon comes up, the flapping *Daily Mails* blow into the lagoon. Torcello is itself again.

No doubt the tourists do spoil it. It is too small, its charm is too fragile, it should not be exposed to such an invasion. The inhabitants bitterly resent the crowds which do a lot of damage and bring very little cash. The inn, though it has wonderfully kept its character, only functions as a real village pub in the evening, and then not always. Parties of rich people come in motor-boats to dine there; make a noise; keep everybody awake until all hours.

The problems observed at Torcello are, in a general way, those of tourism as a whole. It is clearly not a desirable human development, is rapidly getting out of hand, and leads to dislike and misunderstanding between countries. The natives hate the tourists for being (apparently) rich and mean. The tourists despise the natives for being (apparently) poor and feckless. Exterior signs of riches vary so much in different parts of the world that people are often mistaken as to the true state of affairs. A farmer in France or Italy may be very rich indeed, but feel no desire for a smartly-tiled kitchen or well-appointed bathroom. A fur-coated American may not be the millionairess that she seems. Most tourists nowadays pay a sum down for the tour itself, organized in every detail by a travel agency; they may have very little cash to spend on extras. But the native does not realize this. His town is overrun while few compensating advantages come his way. He does not see the tourist as an interesting visitor from another clime but as a purse, and a tight purse at that, containing the deutschmark, the pound, or the dollar. There is nothing to be done about it, impossible to stem the tide, but what will happen when it is swollen by the li, the rouble, the yen, and the rupee? That, far more surely than any war, will be the end of old Europe.

1959

The Great Little Duke

THE bicentenary of the Duc de Saint-Simon's death has been celebrated in Paris by a splendid exhibition at the Bibliothèque Nationale and by many learned essays in the literary papers. In the bookshops two new studies by M. de La Varende and M. Bastide (the last a particularly excellent little introduction) and, for bibliophiles, Pierre Gaxotte's *Scènes et Portraits* are all available, and so are four volumes of the Pléiade edition, taking us up to the death of Louis XIV.

The English have not treated him so well. True, Mr Desmond Flower's translation of a few passages is still in print. But Sir Harold Nicolson and Mr W. H. Lewis, both of whom quote largely from him in their *Good Behaviour* and *The Sunset of the Splendid Century*, seem to regard him respectively as a clever little bore and a gifted liar. He does not really please Englishmen. No Scott-Moncrieff has ever sat down to make an English classic of him. Our nineteenth-century historians and critics hardly mention him. Lord Macaulay does, indeed, speak of 'those inestimable memoirs', but this is the very least he could say, since some of his own most living passages are almost exactly translated from them. He wrote no essay on the Duke—unfortunately, as it would have been so funny. 'It is indeed difficult to conceive how anything short of the rage of hunger should

have induced men to bear the misery of being associates of
the Great King': we can imagine the rolling, sarcastic
sentences. Macaulay, like most of his fellow countrymen,
despised courtiers and had no great love for 'the vain,
the voluptuous but high-spirited French'. In his *Lectures
on Modern History,* Lord Acton only mentions the Duke as
an habitué of La Trappe, not the most characteristic thing
about him. Those who read the *Mémoires* in the highly
inaccurate early editions must have been puzzled by some of
the statements: 'Chamillart, adoré de ses ennemis [commis].'
Oh! the unstable French! Grave faults of transcription
occurred in all the editions until Chéruel's appeared in
1858. But, in any case, no incomprehension is greater than
that of Victorian England for Saint-Simon's France. The
barrier between our two countries, of languages expressing
in almost the same words such different methods of
thought, was reinforced by the gulf between the centuries.
Nineteenth-century Englishmen, like modern Russians and
Americans, thought that life should have a purpose and
works of literature a message. Even Sir Harold Nicolson,
who blossomed in the 1920s, jolliest of men, can never
repress a note of stern disapproval when he mentions the
French Court. 'Lounging courtiers, chattering rubbish',
he says of Saint-Simon and his friends, 'lolling in the foetid
ante-rooms of Versailles.'

In fact, the courtiers at Versailles had but little time for
lounging and lolling; their lives were carefully ordered by
the King so that they must ever be dashing from one part of
the Palace to another, to attend the various functions. True,
Saint-Simon, 'un peu disgracié, pas trop disgracié, juste assez
pour être historien' (Taine) had no job, and only remained
at Versailles because his wife had one. But he was not a

lounger. It was scribble, scribble, scribble all day, in a
mousehole of a room without windows. Over 3,000 large
exercise books were removed from his house in the rue de
Grenelle after his death. They contained his observations
on such subjects as '*l'Ambassade d'Espagne*', filling sixty-
two exercise books, '*Le Mariage de Monsieur avec Mlle de
Montpensier*,' filling fourteen; memoranda, letters to
important people and so on. His *Mémoires*, which have
never been printed in full, cover 2,700 folio pages in his
tight little hand, with no stops, chapters or divisions of any
sort. Like a journalist, he had a passion for hot news;
unlike a journalist, he reported it and then put it away. 'He
who would write the story of his times,' he said, 'truthfully,
and with no respect for persons, should never show it to
anybody. He should leave it to ripen under lock and key.'

That his subject was the Court of France, at a time when
the Court was France, has blinded some of his readers to
the fact that he was by no means a typical courtier. He had
inherited from his father a perfect incapacity to cringe,
bow, stoop and kneel. Duke Claude was one of the old-
fashioned nobles whose backs had not yet been broken by
Louis XIV; stubborn, and eccentric as an English lord. His
son tells us that, something having displeased him in the
Mémoires de La Rochefoucauld, he went off to the bookshop
and scribbled 'The author has lied' in the margins of all the
copies on sale. He had been Master of the Horse to Louis
XIII, who gave him his title of Duc et Pair, and he did not
appreciate the subsequent régime. He retired to Blaye, of
which he was governor, and hardly appeared at the Court of
Louis XIV. His hobby was genealogy, especially his own,
and in the Saint-Simon exhibition there were documents
which belonged to him, purporting to show that the family

descended from Eude l'Insensé and other desirably royal
figures. He died at the age of 87. Next day his young son of
18 came to pay his court at Versailles; as he approached the
throne, Monsieur, the King's brother, said in a loud voice,
'Here we have M. le Duc de Saint-Simon.' They had him
indeed and owe him immortality.

When a small child, Saint-Simon's favourite treats were
royal funerals and requiem masses. He also dearly loved to
interrogate venerable Dukes on questions of precedence
and usage. He was perfectly conversant with the ways of the
Court, but, his father's son, he could never keep quiet if
shocked or displeased by something. He knew that the
King must be treated 'like a god, like a father, like a
mistress', but he could not bring himself to do so. He would
burst out, and the King was for ever telling him to hold his
tongue. He was an agitator, with a purpose and a message.
He wished to be the chronicler of his age and confided his
ambition to M. de Rancé during a retreat at La Trappe.
Encouraged by the approval of the great and holy man he
dedicated his life to this purpose. As for his message, which
could be summarized as Up the Dukes and Down the
Bastards, nothing has ever been so misunderstood. It was
often couched in the snobbish language of his time, so that
he appears to have been concerned only with tiny details of
precedence, but it was really the last kick of the French
aristocracy, the last attempt to keep some power in the
hands of the nobles and prevent them from turning into the
elegant, unreal figures described by Proust. It was a misfortune for France that this message was only partially
heard. Saint-Simon downed the Bastards, which was
immaterial because their male posterity died out almost at
once, but the Dukes had lost the desire to lead, except in

battle. Urged on by him, the Regent tried to restore aristocratic government in France; the aristocrats would not
play and the idea was abandoned for ever. Saint-Simon
failed as a politician. But oh, how he succeeded as a writer!

He was lucky in having such interesting people to write
about as the Bourbon family. Licentious or bigoted, noble
or ignoble, there has seldom been a dull Bourbon. They
were nearly all odd, original men of strong passions,
unaccountable in their behaviour. What could have been
odder and more noble than the steady refusal of Louis XVI
to allow one drop of French blood to be shed, thereby
sealing his own fate and that of his wife and children. What
odder and more ignoble than the cry of Louis XIII on the
day that the adored Cinq-Mars was executed: 'Aha, dit-il,
ce matin à la même heure notre cher ami a passé un mauvais
moment.' Bourbons steal the picture whenever they are in
it. In any account of Marie-Antoinette, Louis XVI becomes
the principal figure: Mme de Pompadour is eclipsed by her
lover and Louis XIV casts a dazzling glare on the pages of all
the writers of the day. He was the oddest member of this
extraordinary family, one of the oddest men who ever lived,
and he is the central character in Saint-Simon's great book.
After his death it becomes very much less interesting,
though Saint-Simon himself, as a member of the Regency
Council, was a more important person.

The Duc du Maine would have seemed dull to us had it
not been for Saint-Simon and his rages against the false,
proud, cowardly, ambitious, devilish, club-footed Bastard.
According to M. de La Varende, Saint-Simon has so blackened Maine that, although we live in an age when rehabilita-
tions are the fashion, nobody has ever attempted to
rehabilitate him. This was written before Mr Lewis's half-

hearted attempt to do so appeared. Mr Lewis could have saved his breath to blow his porridge. It is no good telling us that we must not believe the little, naughty, obstinate Duke, we cannot help believing him. The people of his pages are created for us by him. Maine may have been a brave and competent soldier, a credit to his old father, but it is waste of time to say so. We will as soon believe that Mr Micawber was a sound businessman. Of course, Saint-Simon had his prejudices, but they were usually based on truth; his views seem to have been very just. Violent as were his feelings about the royal Bastards, he had nothing but praise for the charming Comte de Toulouse. He stood by the Duc d' Orléans when all France, most unfairly, believed him to be a poisoner. He was right to hate (while admiring) the King and Mme de Maintenon, who did so much harm to the French aristocracy and therefore to France, and right to love the Bourgognes while fully aware of their curious faults.

Saint-Simon's greatest popular successes, what might be called his anthology pieces, are all concerned with the royal family, and mostly with their deaths. In a way it is a pity that the *Mémoires* should lend themselves so easily to the selection of passages. These are often read while what Lytton Strachey calls 'the enormous panorama, magnificent, palpitating, alive' is left unseen. The day-to-day chronicle is at least as important as the set pieces, which, of course, gain by being read in their proper context. The whole work, to be sure, is immensely long, but it has something for everybody. A Spanish grandee of my acquaintance, not the most bookish man in the world, has often told me of the joy with which he reads and re-reads the chapter on *les grands d'Espagne*. There are, throughout, more genealogical details than are quite fashionable nowadays. But

'He was lucky in having such interesting people to write about as
the Bourbon family.'

nobody says the Bible is a bore because of the pages in which So-and-so begat So-and-so; in the *Mémoires* these details do at least concern people whose descendants we know. Sir Harold Nicolson (who, I see, has got rather under my skin with his sly digs at my favourite) says that he would sooner have Prince Florizel than the Duc de Saint-Simon. It is rather a strange comparison to make, like that, out of the blue. Florizel seems to have been the sort of cheerful young fellow who grows on many a tree, and personally I would gladly trade this Prince for this Duke.

1955

P.S. Since I wrote this, the first volume of *Saint Simon at Versailles* has appeared, a masterly selection and translation from the *Mémoires* by Miss Lucy Norton.

Portrait of a French Country House

I ALWAYS spend the autumn in a French country house which I will call the Château de Sainte Foy. I look forward to this visit all the year; the weeks pass much too quickly; it is a happy time.

Sainte Foy is a long, low white house, like that in *Les Malheurs de Sophie*. It occupies one side of a square on the other side of which are farm buildings; the whole surrounds the basse-cour, where lively, noisy peasants in blue overalls, horses and big wooden farm carts, a herd of cows, tractors and the farmer's own little motor go endlessly to and fro under a tower which dates from the time of Henri IV. In front of the house there is a wooded park intersected by canals, containing two ancient chapels, a dovecote, a kitchen garden and a charmille or hornbeam avenue without which no French park is complete.

An important convent which stood here until the Revolution was razed to the ground; the house remained; it was built in the eighteenth century to put up the friends and relations of the nuns. Perhaps this is why it is such a perfect place for guests. Its owner, Mme de Florange, fills it with people whenever she is there; so did her parents before her; for a century Sainte Foy (unchanged, except that now every bedroom has its bathroom) has sheltered a cheerful company.

Many of my fellow guests have been coming here ever

since they were born, as their parents came before them. They keep the same rooms and leave various belongings from one visit to another. Impossible to convey the prettiness of these rooms, with their old-fashioned furniture, amateur water-colours and double taffeta curtains, pink and white. They are all on the east front, away from the farmyard, the only manifestation of which is an occasional rich whiff of manure. At night one hears the owls, the noise, like rain, of wind in the poplars and the thud of walnuts falling from the tree.

I arrive at Sainte Foy on September 1. It is one o'clock and the party is gathered among the orange tubs in front of the house. There are cries of joy, hugs; cares and bothers fall away—for many weeks now we shall be free of them. The atmosphere at Sainte Foy is very much like that in a Russian play—endless chat, endless leisure, a little plotting, secrets in the charmille; the difference is that ennui does not exist. (In all the years I have lived in France I have never come across it, although in the eighteenth century people here were eaten by it.)

The house party, as in Russian plays, is composed of disparate elements, young and old, egg-heads and bone-heads, saints and sinners, grasshoppers and ants. We are seldom fewer than eight or more than twelve. A grave element is provided by one or two Abbés, a learned lady who knows all about medieval architecture, and the tutor of Mme de Florange's grandchildren. They regard Mrs H., M. d'Albano, aged ninety-five, M. de La Tour and myself as agreeable but weightless.

M. d'Albano composes definitions: 'Yes. Ne veut vraiment dire oui . . . qu'à toutes choses anglaises.' 'Héros.

Beaucoup ne tiennent pas à l'etre mais combien voudraient l'avoir été.'

M. de La Tour restores pictures and has turned a blackened canvas on the staircase into a (perhaps) Bassano —I sometimes wish he hadn't, the head of St. John the Baptist is so very unpleasant. He is a Chekov character, young, romantic, elusive, elegant and rather mysterious; he desperately loves the beauty of this world and feels the approach of an engulfing tide of ugliness which he doubts being able to survive. This makes him melancholy.

Cares and bothers fall away at Sainte Foy, but not for Mrs H., since caring and bothering are her hobbies; she exudes a sort of frivolous pessimism which nobody takes very seriously. She is the most French English person I know. Her father was on the staff of Lord Lyons and she was born at the Paris embassy, in the same room, though not at the same time, as Mr Somerset Maugham. They bowled their hoops together in the Tuileries gardens. She first came to Sainte Foy when she was six weeks old; her girlhood was spent between the banks of the Thames and the banks of the Marne; when she married she made a centre for the intellectual element in London society. She has a tragic greenish face with huge black eyes, and dresses in the colours of mourning. She said to me once 'Child' (I am *Child* to her and *La Petite* to Mme de Florange, it is so agreeable) 'Child, you should never put any make-up on your face—artists do not admire it'. 'All very well for you' I said 'since you look like El Greco's mistress. If I put no make-up on I look like an old English governess.' While the others are greeting me with every appearance of satisfaction, Mrs H., whom I have not seen for months, only says 'Have you brought a paper, Child? No paper? Of course, you care nothing for the break-up of civilization.'

For some reason civilization always seems nearer its break-up in September than at any other time of year, an added reason for spending that fidgety month at Sainte Foy, where the sound of drums is muffled. No daily paper is seen there, except the English ones which Mrs H. and I receive by post, two days late. 'As you have the *Daily Telegraph*, Child, I will arrange to have *The Times*'. There is an antique wireless in the drawing-room, but it gives a powerful electric shock to anybody rash enough to turn it on.

None of us minds not knowing the latest news except Mrs H. who, gloomily fascinated by the break-up of civilization, simply longs for a peep into the present. At the time of Suez I used to take pity on her and manipulate the wireless with an india-rubber. 'This is the end!' Like all English people she and I took sides over Suez and furious were our arguments. The French rather agreed about its being the end, but they did not fly at each other's throats—they shrugged their shoulders and blamed the Americans.

Mme de Florange is a tall, beautiful, elegant woman, born the same year as Sir Winston Churchill, Dr Adenauer and the late Pope. Like them she is extremely authoritarian; the world has always been at her feet and she gets her own way. She happens to be a saint. Saints are seldom easy of commerce; Mme de Florange resembles the eagle rather than the dove. She is a rebel and something of a pheno-menon; in her world, Catholic, royalist, *bien pensant*, Action Française, it is most unusual to be, as she is, a firm Gaullist. The cry generally goes up: 'I vote for the General with both my hands so as to avoid shaking his.' They vote for him because 'who else is there?' But they hate.

Mme de Florange, and this too is unlike many of her compatriots, is full of fantasy. Impossible to guess how she will take things. She is not shocked by Voltaire or Anatole France (though the children are not allowed to read them) or even by Mendès-France; she positively enjoys *L'Express* for its vile cleverness. She has always been interested in contemporary art, was painted by Cubists and made great friends with Bonnard, who gave her a picture. Somebody once found the list of people she prays for every day—in among the family names there were Louis XIV and Landru. 'Poor man,' she said when asked why Landru, 'it seems he has no relations to pray for him.' Exceedingly religious, she spends more time in church than in the drawing-room. She is not with the others when I arrive; her maid is on her way to the Chapel to tell her that luncheon is ready.

Meanwhile Mrs H., who came from England an hour ago, is recounting her news, all bad. 'My doctor I was so fond of has gone into broilers.' 'Broilairs? Qu'est ce que c'est que ça?' 'A kind of chicken you keep in the dark and feed with injections. He says they can't ring him up in the night— oh, it is too hard.'

'But these broilairs must be very nasty?' They are more concerned with the sufferings of the consumer than those of the hen.

'Oh, very. But nobody cares. Veal in England now tastes of blotting-paper—why? Because the calves live in Turkish baths,' she adds, conjuring up a picture of Hamams all over England's green and pleasant land.

The day begins at Sainte Foy, as in all French houses, by the noise, like pistol shots, of wooden shutters being thrown back. Not mine. I sleep with everything open, so I love the French window which marries a house to the firmament instead of dividing them like the stuffy sash.

Soon Mme Congis appears with coffee and croissants. She lives, with lucky, lucky M. Congis, in a village some miles away; comes pedalling over on her bicycle before breakfast and leaves again after tea, laden with black-edged letters for the post. She is passionately interested in the goings-on at Sainte Foy; having dumped the tray on one's knee, she folds her arms, says 'Voilà!' and then makes an announcement.

'Voilà! M. l'Abbé Fesch got on to one of the children's donkeys after Mass, for a joke, and has been carried away over the hill. Mme la Comtesse is most worried.'

'Voilà! Meeses H. has got raging toothache and she is going now to the dentist at Meaux.' All heads out of all windows as the motor is heard; Mrs H., wrapped in shawls, emerges from the house, looks up like a Gothic saint, cries, 'Pray for me' and is driven off to her martyrdom.

Once a year Mme Congis announces: 'Voilà! Madame knows that tomorrow is Bishop's Day?' Everybody enjoys this. Monseigneur, who is a great dear, comes, with his chaplain, and says Mass at nine o'clock. After a vast breakfast for all the tenants he retires to a room put at his disposal and does his morning's work. Luncheon is a gargantuan feast attended by many priests (some of whom come from Paris) and neighbours. The women all curtsy to the Bishop and kiss his ring. Madame de Florange's beautiful English daughter-in-law once met him unexpectedly in the charmille. He held out his ringed hand—she took it absent-mindedly and said 'Oh, what a pretty stone!' At the luncheon table where, like a king, he acts as host, the foreigners, Mrs H. and I sit on each side of him and she

144

pumps him for all she is worth about civilization's break-up. But he is a jolly, optimistic character to whom the next world is more real than this one; Nasser and the Bomb leave him singularly unmoved. After luncheon he and the other priests sit drinking coffee, smoking, chatting and laughing. They look like a picture of the Cardinal School.

André the butler comes into his own on the Bishop's Day, which is largely organized by him. He is an adorable man. A walking encyclopaedia, he suffers, at meals, from loose statements of uncertain facts. Sometimes his lips move frantically as he tries, without actually speaking, to prompt some hesitating speaker.

'Who came after Sadi Carnot?' M. de La Tour said, vaguely. That evening he found a neat list of the Presidents of the Republic, and their dates, on his dressing-table. At dinner a fellow guest, shouting at a deaf lady, said: 'La rue de Tilsit—Tilsit comme la bataille.' I couldn't resist saying in a know-all voice: 'There was no battle at Tilsit.' 'Will you bet?' Fortified by a nod from André, I betted and won 100 francs. Coming down early for dinner one often finds him looking up something in Larousse. If I sit down absent-mindedly before some visiting Abbé has said grace, André gives me a sharp thump on the back. Somebody once asked what he would like for a Christmas present and he replied, 'A love poem by Alfred de Vigny, framed.'

His predecessor was a Moor called Mahmoud who had been condemned to death by his compatriots and therefore never wanted a day off. However, he fell, with lustful intent, upon Bernadette the between-maid and had to be sacked. Soon afterwards poor Mahmoud was found with his throat cut.

On Friday various men who work in Paris come down

145

en weekend. Mrs H. awaits them as if they were the Messiah, hoping to glean much information on current affairs. Indeed, they are full of it and soon she knows exactly what is being said at the Jockey Club. It seldom tallies with what she sees in her *New Statesman and Nation*, so she tries to arrive at some truth half-way between the two.

They bring heaps of newspapers, sweets and flowers for Mme de Florange (in France flowers are taken to, not from the country) and any new books which the authors happen to have given them. Most of the books lying about on the drawing-room table are written by dukes and duchesses. This does not mean that we are down to society memoirs; there are some highbrow French dukes; three of them are in the French Academy, where they may soon be joined by the Duchesse de La Rochefoucauld as the first woman member.

When people ask me what I do all day at Sainte Foy I am at a loss to reply. I only know that the time seems to be crammed with delightful ploys and that I never can count on doing any work there. We pose for Mme de Florange, who paints enormous, masterly altar-pieces. We have all figured in these as angels or devils or victims of the plague.

We play a good deal of bridge. The visit always begins with me imploring our hostess to allow us to play for two sous instead of one. 'Certainly not. We have always played here for one sou and we always shall.' She is a wild over-bidder and hates winning. Mrs H. is a wild underbidder and hates losing. 'Child, you always win except when you are playing with me, it is so hard.' We have furious struggles and acid arguments, sometimes ending in a telephone call to a friend of Albarron in Paris to settle the matter.

Incidentally the farmers in this part of Seine et Marne are

terrible gamblers. The Mayor of Pouy, who has one of the biggest farms in the district, often comes to play with us (for one sou). He tells of really mad poker games; one of his colleagues recently lost a team of horses to another—they were sent over the next morning, their carter in floods of tears. This charming Mayor takes me and M. de La Tour every year to the forest of Ermenonville to hear the stags roaring under a full moon. The forest is full of creatures crashing about, the stags sound like lions, it all seems as primitive as the Congo and yet is less than an hour's drive from Paris.

Sainte Foy is plumb in the battlefield of the Marne; the two wars are still the chief topic of conversation between the peasants and a foreigner like myself. They had a bad time here with the Germans and show no enthusiasm at all for United Europe. There is a touching little book, printed locally after the first war, telling exactly what happened to the inhabitants of five neighbouring villages in the autumn of 1914.

The Mayor of Pouy has fascinating stories of the Battle of the Marne, in which he fought as a very young man. He will never forget how one morning, after several nights of no sleep for anybody, he saw an Indian officer calmly sitting by the road while an orderly wound his turban. He says the mules of the Indian regiment always looked as if they had just that minute been polished. In this district the English are regarded as faithful brothers in arms; Mers el Kebir and our (real or imagined) behaviour, hostile to France, in Arab lands have made no impact here. In 1943 M. Gouasc, Mme de Florange's farmer, hid an English captain for many months and received a constant flow of 'parachutages'. Gouasc was finally caught, taken to Germany and died as a result of his treatment there. The Captain got away; he was finally killed in Burma. '*Le pauvre Capitaine—il était bien gentil.*' When the peasants tell you these things they extol each other's behaviour but never speak of their own.

One of my fellow guests who was a girl in 1914 was doing her embroidery in a little summer house, which we still use, perched up on the park wall like a bird's nest, when suddenly she saw Uhlans galloping over the hill. In those early days with the armies on the move, there was often no means of knowing that the enemy was near. The family then went to Paris, leaving Sainte Foy in the charge of their groom. A few days later a German officer rode up the drive, made straight for the harness room and helped himself to a bridle. He asked the groom 'where are M. de Florange and M. d'Albano?' 'With their regiments.' He spoke about one or two other friends of the house and then went off down a path across the fields which no stranger could have found. Who was this mysterious person? None of them knew any German officer. So it is thought that the children's Fraulein must have been a man all along—she always looked like one they say and had a distinct moustache.

There are lovely walks at Sainte Foy. You can go over the uplands, past the corn ricks and the old windmill to Pouy, which consists of a dozen white-washed houses, with red and blue roofs, clustering round a Romanesque church; down a dusty white lane, bordered by nuts and black-berries, to Mareilly, where the village shop can sometimes provide a copy of *L'Aurore*, or through a poplar wood to the watercress beds.

When M. de La Tour was restoring a naïve fresco in Pouy church I used to go up there, after tea, and walk home with him. Like many French people, he pretends to regard his compatriots as worse than idiotic, 'The boobies (*cré-tins*)—what do they care about their beautiful church?' So it was a pleasant surprise when he received a round robin from all the parishioners thanking him for his trouble.

When I first knew this country, just after the war, the aspect of the villages was decidedly grubby, but lately there has been an improvement, due, I think, to a few Parisian weekenders who have bought cottages. The town mouse has taught the country mouse to paint his woodwork, hang pretty curtains, cook on Butagaz, and plant flowers in his garden. Perhaps everybody is richer now, but I believe lack of imagination, rather than of cash, was often responsible for the old sad look. This year I noticed one or two washing-machines but I have yet to see a television set.

The farms in this part of France are large enough to be prosperous. The chief crops are wheat, maize, and beet. Modern appliances are used more and more; at Sainte Foy the forty Friesian cows are milked and fenced in by electricity; there is a big Ferguson tractor and other motorized equipment; but Champagne, a dear white horse, who loves his carter so much that he watches him all the time, like a dog, and Jean-Mermoz, a nappy old chestnut, still do a lot of work. The French consider that horses are useful when the soil is wet, they produce manure and can eventually be eaten, none of which can be said for the tractor.

A horrible manifestation of the modern world, hitherto so remote, came to Sainte Foy last year. Some clever young Civil Servants arrived in a caravan to prospect for oil. They dug an enormous crater in a wheat field just outside the park wall and set up a pump which made a deafening noise night and day; powerful searchlights glared behind the trees; the whole effect was hellish. We were warned that if oil was found, a shanty town would spring up on the pastures; the atmosphere would be laden with petrol; the pump and the searchlights become a permanence. Furthermore, Mme de Florange and young M. Gouasc, her farmer, would receive a tiny sum in compensation, but not a penny of profit, because, since long before the Revolution, everything under the earth in France has belonged to the State. Mercifully the prospectors drew a blank. They gave the farmer £100 for temporarily ruining his field, filled in the crater, and moved off to find a substantial layer of oil some twelve miles away.

Sainte Foy was saved, but for how long? Near as it is to Paris, will it not soon become part of the *agglomération Parisienne*? Will all the clever, handsome peasants be crammed into factories to make unnecessary objects for the use of other peasants in other factories? Will the poplar trees be cut down to be replaced by Unités, i.e. blocks of flats with their own shops and swimming baths, rising out of concrete car parks?

Perhaps not, after all. I really cannot imagine Mme Congis or the Mayor of Pouy living in a Unité.

PS. I showed this account of Sainte Foy to a French friend who said, 'My dear, if the English think we all live like this, they will never join the Common Market.' I said, 'Don't worry at all, the English don't believe a word I tell them; they regard me as their chief purveyor of fairy tales.'

1961.

NANCY MITFORD, born in 1904, the eldest of the seven Mitfords, was an enormously successful and popular novelist and biographer called "devastatingly witty" and "one of Britain's most piercing observers of social manners" by the *New York Times.* Her novels *The Pursuit of Love* and *Love in a Cold Climate* are among the funniest of our time and have been in print continuously since their publication over thirty-five years ago. After writing seven novels she moved to history with a biography of Madame de Pompadour and, several years later, a study of Louis XIV called *The Sun King,* followed by biographies of Voltaire and Frederick the Great. These books prompted Louis Auchincloss to comment in 1969, "She seems to have brought a new talent to the study of history, that of the sophisticated, worldly wise observer who is able to penetrate old archives with a fresh eye for qualities in the dead that she is specially qualified to recognize." Nancy Mitford died at her house in Versailles in 1973.